# Displaced

A MODERN BALTIC SAGA

The cataclysmic forces that in 1944 drove young Juris and his immediate family from their Latvian homeland, coincided with the widespread destruction and reshaping of virtually the entire European geopolitical landscape. This account is a glimpse of those calamitous events as they impacted the life of one small boy from Riga.

"A young man's ultimate triumph over two of the world's most cruel and ruthless dictatorships…"

Copyright © 2021 William Gemmell, All Rights Reserved.

This work is a retelling of actual events that occurred during the life of its subject Juris "George" Meija, as recalled and recounted by him in later life, including his impressions and opinions of the events as they occurred. Some aspects of the subject's real-life memories and opinions may be disturbing to certain individuals. Reader discretion is advised.

Displaced — a Modern Baltic Saga

Published by Road to Obi ABN 98 149 004 689

PO Box 58 Mapleton Queensland 4560 Australia

Copyright © 2021, 2022 by William Gemmell

All rights reserved. No part of this book may be scanned, uploaded, reproduced, distributed or transmitted in any form or by any means whatsoever without the written permission of the author, except in the case of brief quotations embodied in critical articles and reviews. Thank you for supporting the Author's rights.

First Published 2022.

Worldwide printing and distribution by Ingram Spark.

https://www.ingramspark.com

ISBN 978-0-646-86011-4

*Juris aged 15, alive and free in the shadow of the Sydney Harbour Bridge, 1950.*

*Displaced — A Modern Baltic Saga.*

# Contents

## Prologue — 4

## 1. Intrusions — 10

- 1.1 Where it began — 11
- 1.2 Our Year of Terror — 15
- 1.3 Nazi Invasion — 21
- 1.4 What We Knew — 26

## 2. Taking Flight — 27

- 2.1 Goodbye to Riga — 30
- 2.2 A Narrow Passage — 32
- 2.3 The Forge of Life — 35

## 3. Drittes Reich — 39

- 3.1 The End in Sight — 41
- 3.2 A Welcome Respite — 43
- 3.3 Fiery Retribution — 47
- 3.4 Final Skirmish — 53

## 4. Self Reparation — 57

- 4.1 Finding Our Feet — 59
- 4.2 Emigrants — 61
- 4.3 A Fishy Beginning — 64

## 5. Up and Away — 67

- 5.1 Viva Adelaide — 69
- 5.2 Those Salad Days — 73
- 5.3 Student Shenanigans — 79

## 6. Fully Fledged — 83

- 6.1 Military Madness — 85
- 6.2 Feats of Engineering — 90

## 7. Full Circle — 93

- 7.1 Return to Riga — 95
- 7.2 Mistrusted — 96
- 7.3 The Boot Factory — 98
- 7.4 Man vs The Machine — 100
- 7.5 A Rocky Road — 102
- 7.6 Fraternity — 103
- 7.7 Where to, Latvia? — 105
- 7.8 The Price to Pay — 107

## 8. Epilogue — 109

- 8.1 Quest for Happiness — 111
- 8.2 Relationships — 112
- 8.3 The Finer Things — 113
- 8.4 Engagement — 114
- 8.6 Accomplishment — 115
- 8.7 Purpose — 116
- 8.8 A Final Word — 117

# Displaced
### A MODERN BALTIC SAGA

## Preface

Why? In the first place, there's the record. For years, my friend George has regaled me with occasional glimpses into his brainbox full of engaging, amusing and sometimes hair-raising exploits, to the extent where, with both of us getting on in age, we realised it was time to set some of them down in a form less volatile than oral tradition, or even digital code.

Secondly, not much seems to have been recorded from an individual perspective about the Latvian experience of displacement in World War Two, and how those overwhelming events impacted the lives of thousands of ordinary Latvian people. In particular, how a young boy and his family suffered the horrors of war in Europe, and eventually took to a new life in Australia. From war-traumatised child to graduate engineer, business leader, entrepreneur, international economic advisor, business mentor, and long-serving Honorary Consul — it's a story that deserves to be told.

I am honoured that George chose me to be his voice. I hope that my efforts provide a measure of both insight and context to his extraordinary escapades.

William Gemmell
Blackall Range, Queensland 2021

*Displaced — A Modern Baltic Saga.*

# Foreword

Dear Readers, it's almost expected these days to hear younger people complain, barely three generations after the most depraved war our world has ever witnessed, about how difficult or deprived their lives are, when their Wifi connection fails, or when their pizza arrives with the wrong topping.

I asked my friend Bill to help me set down this encapsulation of my life's recollections, not only because I believe it's important not to forget how quickly an ostensibly civilised society can descend into chaos, but also because I love Latvia, the land of my ancestors. Having been compulsorily ejected from there as a child, I hope to leave behind my personal account of the kind of place I believe my homeland once was, and hopefully will become again.

*Dedicated to my wonderful grandaughters, Emily and Kate Meija, with my love.*

Latvia is a small but beautiful country with a long, complex and proud history. I hope this narrative serves to convey an adequate sense of our inherited traditions, our spirit, and our values, which despite the prolonged and disastrously deleterious efforts of infinitely more powerful neighbours, we have yet managed to retain.

Juris Sigurds "George" Meija
Brisbane, Australia 2021

The national flag of Latvia was adopted by Independent Latvia in 1918 and used until the young nation's first occupation by Soviet Russia in 1940. The flag's display was prohibited during the subsequent periods of Soviet and German occupation. In February 1990, after 50 years in the shadows, shortly before our country regained its independence from the USSR, the new Latvian government re-adopted the nation's original standard, depicted above.

# Prologue.

The cataclysmic forces that in 1944 drove young Juris and his immediate family from their Latvian homeland, coincided with the widespread destruction and reshaping of virtually the entire European geopolitical landscape. This account is a glimpse of those calamitous events as they impacted the life of one small boy from Riga.

Long before the 1917 Russian Revolution and the 1933 rise of Nazi Germany, Latvia had maintained centuries-old traditional links with both Germany and Imperial Russia, due to the nation's Baltic coastal location and the trading prosperity of its capital city, Riga.

Following the 1918 Russian Revolution, the Latvian people had emphatically asserted their rejection of communism and their right to self-rule by winning a brief armed struggle against Soviet Russia and the Bolsheviks' short-lived Latvian Socialist Soviet Republic. The Riga Peace Treaty of 1920 established the independent Republic of Latvia.

Latvia's independence proved problematic however. The unfolding collision between Nazi Germany's territorial designs and the expansionist ambitions of Soviet Russia produced high-level wrangling between those two increasingly belligerent powers. Not least, their secret negotiations produced the 1939 Molotov-Ribbentrop Pact involving an arrangement that divided future governance of various territories, including Latvia, between Nazi Germany and the Soviet Union.

World War Two erupted in 1939 when Nazi Germany seized Poland. In the wake of Germany's successful invasion, the Soviets declared that the nation of Poland had 'effectively ceased to exist' and they too crossed the Soviet-Polish frontier, claiming the need to protect Belarusians and Ukrainians in the region.

The next months and years saw Latvia invaded first by the Soviets in 1940, then in 1941 by Nazi Germany, and then again by the Soviets in 1944.

The bitter ideological struggles between Soviet Russia and Nazi Germany produced a large-scale and widespread military conflict, resulting in occupations and relinquishments of various territories such as Latvia, accompanied on both sides by enforced upheavals, mass murders, resettlements, and movements of ethnic and other populations.

The countless disruptions and human tragedies that resulted from these overwhelming political events were beyond the control of ordinary citizens. In most cases, the predominant strategy for people throughout Europe was to do and say whatever was necessary to support their individual struggles to survive.

Millions of Europeans, including Juris' parents, were forced by their political circumstances, including the threat of execution, to cooperate with whichever regime was in power.

In the event, the 1944 Soviet return to Latvia caused thousands to flee ahead of an irresistible Red Army advance. The departure from Riga of nine-year-old Juris and his immediate family became part of that great exodus, and where his greatest adventures began.

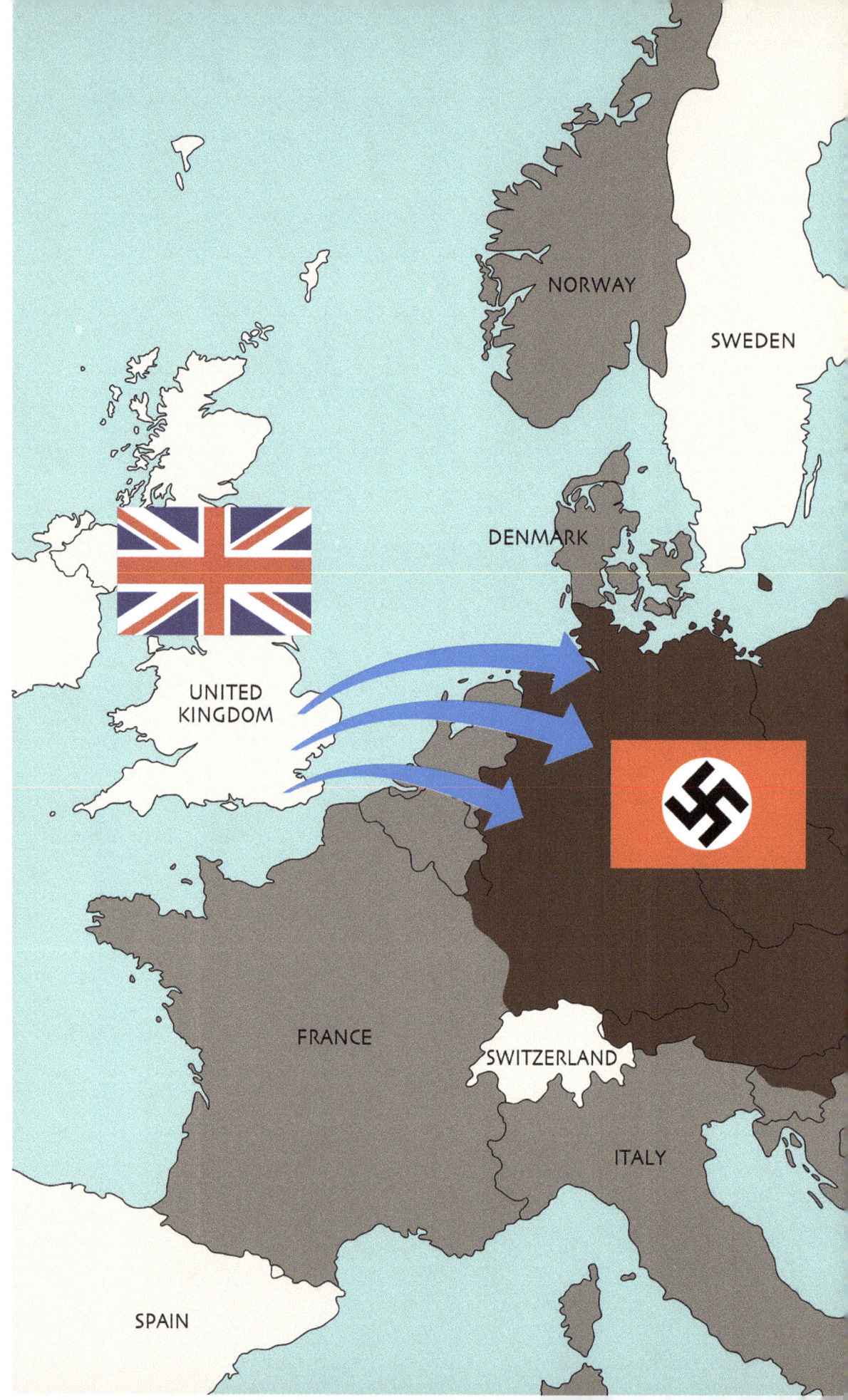

*Displaced – A Modern Baltic Saga.*

# 1

PART ONE

# 1
# Intrusions.

*Today Riga would be readily recognisable to Juri's parents and grandparents.*

## 1.1  Where it Began

These days in Australia they call me 'George,' but I was born Juris Sigurds Meija in January 1935, in the well-ordered and prosperous city of Riga, in the Baltic Republic of Latvia.

Riga is a picturesque city; famous for its distinctive architectural styles, its many old stone and wooden buildings, and its deeply ingrained historical traditions.

We Latvians are proud of our ancient, multicultural, multilingual heritage. Our capital city Riga is located near the mouth of the Daugava River, on the Baltic Sea. The ancestors of our people first settled the region some 5,000 years ago. Those ancient Balts, as our ethnic group are known, established the earliest overland trade routes to the Mediterranean via Byzantium, or modern-day Istanbul, trading local amber and other commodities for precious metals.

Riga provides a calm anchorage some 15 km upstream from the river mouth. As early as 200 AD the site was noted as an important stopover on the Viking cross-continental trading route between the Baltic and Mediterranean Seas.

Later Germanic traders likewise established centuries-old associations with Riga and built a fortified outpost there, as early as 1200 AD.

In more recent centuries, Riga and the Daugava provided an effective and lucrative trading intersection between Imperial Russia and the remainder of Europe.

When I landed in the world, my mother Nadja was a self-employed fashion designer, dressmaker and tailor, operating her own Riga salon for wealthy clientele. She imported the latest modes from Paris and employed women to sew her own designs. Her progress up until that time had not been without its challenges, however.

She had been born Nadja Arnholds in 1903, of Latvian heritage, in the Imperial Russian city of St Petersburg.

Decades earlier, during the 19th century, the Arnholds family had owned a munitions factory in the Latvian town of Jelgava, at a time when the reforming Russian Czar Nicholas was encouraging manufacturers such as the Arnholds to relocate to Russia.

Their factory had been a welcome addition in St Petersburg and for a time the Arnholds family occupied an honoured place in Imperial Russian society — they prospered.

By the age of 19, my mother Nadja had survived not only childhood diphtheria but also the Russian Revolution. In 1922 she managed to evade the Bolsheviks and, with her younger brother Arnold, joined their father Nicolai, in Riga.

Unfortunately, Nicolai fell ill and died within a few months. The young siblings found themselves alone and unsupported, their parents having previously divorced. My grandmother Leonida had earlier chosen to remain in Russia, hoping to fulfil her dream of becoming an opera singer-diva. Later, Arnold moved to Tallin in Estonia, where he married.

The union of my parents grew from a friendship between Nadja and my father's sister Aleksandra, who had visited Nadja's salon on many occasions.

In those days Oskar is said to have cut a dashing figure, having previously served in the Latvian Cavalry during World War One, and later fighting against both Germany and Russia for Latvia's 1920 independence.

*Grandpapa Matis, father Oskar and Juris aged almost three, Christmas time 1937.*

Aleksandra invited Nadja to visit the Meija family farm and there she met Oskar. The rest, as they say, is history — they were soon married.

By the time I was born, Oskar had ascended Latvia's bureaucratic ladder to become our nation's Director of Public Health. Prior to his having risen to this prestigious role, having returned from his wars and obeying the wishes of his father, Oskar had briefly read Agriculture at Riga University.

Uninspired by the agrarian curriculum however, he had abandoned his studies and joined a Farmers' Co-Op as a sales representative, selling Latvian grain and other farming produce as far afield as Denmark.

Those ealy years of my life seeemed idyllic. My parents' careers were flourishing and our family was prosperous.

I was apparently an inquisitive little fellow who wanted to know

*My Mama Nadja (centre), with some of her salon's workers.*

everything. For this reason my parents called me *Kapeec*, or 'Little-why.' They were forever answering my questions, telling me stories, or instructing me.

I remember my father reading to me from an illustrated book in verse, about an animal-market in the countryside. He would point to each word as he read it aloud. In this way, I began reading at two-and-a-half — a surprise to my parents. After that, I read anything I could get my hands on.

My Mama's salon was popular and a significant contributor to our family income. Nadja preferred to have me with her at her work, where she could keep watch over me. Some of my earliest memories were of the happy hours I spent there, amusing myself, observing the goings-on.

It was there that I learned, for example, that from their respective demeanours, men and women are quite different. My place was in the front room where Mama greeted her customers, at a small table with my books and toys. On seeing me there, lady visitors would tend to fuss over me and I would stand dutifully to accept their attentions, usually involving small talk and a hug.

From these encounters it gradually became clear to me that women, unlike men, tended to be soft, squishy and somewhat redolent, and unlike men, were mostly quite uninterested in either my age or in the reading matter at hand.

My masculine interactions, on the other hand, were usually occasioned by a client's husband attending a garment fitting with his wife. They would go something like this:

*A Baltic amber ring from ancient Egypt, declared by expert antiquarians to have originated from a Mycenaean workshop. Amber was believed to not only ward off misfortune, but also to possess the power of healing.*

*A medieval building in Riga's old town, illustrating the city's distinctive architectural traditions.*

*Wife*: "Oh look darling, this is Mrs Meija's little boy Juris. See? He is reading already. What a clever child!"

*Husband*: "Reading? Already? How old are you Juris? That is excellent!"

Usually, husband would then join me in punctilious silence at my small table, perhaps browsing a newspaper — thus demonstrating correct manly deportment.

And so on, as the years gently passed, I gradually increased in awareness. All too soon however, those blissful times were to come crashing down around us.

## 1.2 Our Year of Terror

I was five years old when our tranquil existence was turned upside-down. Soviet Russia invaded in the summer of 1940, easily overpowering our small nation's intrepid yet futile resistance.

Within weeks, Latvia was entirely subjugated. This included the establishment of Soviet military bases, control over every aspect of our lives, and arrival of the NKVD, Stalin's terrifying secret police.

The brutality of this first Russian occupation was the start of the most fearful and turbulent period in our history. While many of my later war experiences were especially difficult, these too are worth retelling.

The countless horrific aspects of the 1940-41 Soviet occupation were such that, even today, it is remembered as Latvia's "Year of Terror."

The invasion came about because those two initially allied, ruthless tyrants Hitler and Stalin, had conspired to divide Poland between them, and for Soviet Russia to annex the Baltic States — Estonia, Latvia and Lithuania.

Precise figures are unavailable for the human losses inflicted on Latvia during that year, from military action, executions, deportations and torture.

It is recorded that in just two days in June 1941, at least 15,600 men, women and children, including 20% of our republic's last legal government, were either murdered or forcibly deported.

In all, it was estimated that 2% of the entire Latvian population vanished without trace, including thousands of Latvian Jews. Many sought refuge abroad, but escape was obviously not a solution available to everyone.

At first, the humiliation and shock of the Soviet invasion was too much for my father, occurring as it had barely two decades after his World War One military service, and his subsequent armed independence struggle against both the Bolsheviks and Germany.

He was struck down with a deep despondency. To his mind, his efforts and the sacrifice of thousands of his young comrades had been for nothing. For what seemed like weeks, he lay in his darkened bedroom, where Nadja cared for and comforted him.

*Russian tanks and troops parading to a mixed reception through the streets of Riga, 1940.*

Eventually, he emerged to face the disaster. He was, after all, our nation's Director of Health and felt duty-bound to see what was happening to his Department. On arriving at his office, he found the building's former janitor, garish hammer and sickle on his arm, pistol on his belt, seated in Oskar's former room, in his Director's chair.

"Ah! Comrade Meija. Enter!" the former janitor commanded.

"As you can see, it is I now in charge. You bourgeois pigs are finished."

"I assure you Comrade," replied Oskar, "that's quite alright with me!"

Barely a week later, our home telephone rang. Nervously, my father answered it and the caller announced, "Comrade Meija, I am Koklachov. I have come from Moscow to organise Latvia's Health Department. You will return to your office, immediately."

Oskar knew he could not refuse. Tears streaming down her face, my Mama said good-bye, believing she would never see her husband again.

Papa hugged me, "Be brave my boy. Look after your Mama."

To our great relief however, in less than an hour, Oskar was home again, a wry grin creasing his face.

He sat with us at the kitchen table and explained what had happened.

He had nervously traversed the two blocks to the Health Department in Lacplesa Street and entered by the lift. By the time he reached his fourth-floor office, acutely aware that the Russians were openly liquidating their so-called 'enemies of the State,' his knees were shaking and he felt queasy.

With great apprehension, he had knocked on the door of his former office and had heard in Russian, "Enter."

There were two men inside, one seated stiffly behind his director's desk, the other standing. The seated man stood, walked around the desk, extended his hand and spoke.

"Comrade Meija! I am Dmitri Koklachov, and this is Comrade Vasily Goldstein, from the NKVD. Thank you for coming so quickly — we appreciate prompt action."

"I do not live far from here..." Oskar had proffered, cautiously.

"Comrade Meija, we know precisely where you live. Be seated, please."

Koklachov sat down again, in Oskar's former chair. The NKVD man stood sternly beside him.

*Displaced — A Modern Baltic Saga.*

"Comrade, I will come straight to the point", said Koklachov.

"We are authorised to offer you a new position, that of Commissar of Health. It is effectively your old job, but we will be here to assist you in adjusting your philosophical outlook to that of the free and democratic Latvian Soviet Republic — a welcome member of the Soviet Union. Because you are literate and fluent in our language, Moscow is of the opinion that you will be ideal."

Oskar had been stunned. He could see a file on his desk with his name on it. So, he thought, they probably know everything about me. They must know that the Meija family had owned a sizeable farm and that we might therefore be considered 'class enemies' — *Kulaks* — to be potentially liquidated. They would likely know also, that Nadja was from a bourgeois family and had absconded from the Russian workers' paradise in 1922.

His mind racing, Oskar muttered something about what an honour the offer was, and might he consider …?

Goldstein interrupted in a threatening tone and a cold manner.

"Consider? What could there possibly be to consider, Comrade?"

"I merely thought..."

"But of course, Comrade — think! This is a free workers' republic. Take your time — relax, think. Citizens are at perfect liberty to decide for themselves. But you would not need more than one or two moments, would you not agree?"

Oskar hesitated and again Goldstein interrupted, this time sharp, aggressive. "Now see here, Comrade, you have a wife and small son, yes? I am sure you appreciate the importance of their wellbeing. So, what is there to consider?"

Oskar appreciated, perfectly.

"Of course, Comrade — I can see now that your offer is both a wonderful opportunity and a privilege. I accept. Indeed, I am honoured. Thank you."

Out came a bottle of Vodka and three large tumblers. Koklachov poured each man a glass, half full.

"To the Soviet Republic and the glory of the Proletariat! Hurrah!" he proclaimed, downing his tumbler's contents in one gulp.

"But, what has happened to our Comrade the janitor?" enquired Oskar.

"The janitor?" Goldstein shrugged.

"Sadly," he said, spreading his fingers,

*Victims of the Soviet 'terror' in Valmiera, many showing the evidence of torture.*

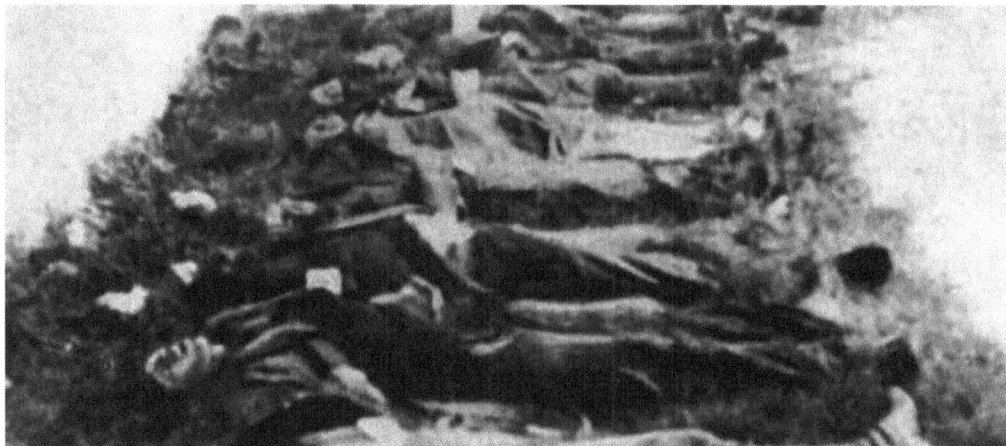

*Soviet authorities constantly proclaimed equality for all, but under the guise of the class struggle, they brought official violence, dividing society according to Marxist socio-economic principles, into oppressors and the oppressed. This policy meant identifying 'class enemies,' leading to arrests, mass deportations and executions. These invariably tended to be swift, carried out with ruthless efficiency by NKVD officers, usually in the dead of night.*

"we were obliged to liquidate him."

"But surely…" Oskar stammered, "He has been a Party Member for ten years; even longer perhaps…"

"Quite so, indeed. But the fellow was deluded — crazed is how I would personally describe it. He mistakenly believed that the Party owed him something — and of course, the Party owes nobody anything…

"It is we, mere humble Citizens, who owe the Party, Comrade!"

"And so," Oskar continued to Nadja and me, "Tomorrow, I am to begin with my new job, that being my old job."

Our family life was to be allowed to continue, at least for the time being.

A minority of Latvians welcomed the Soviet agenda, but most despaired. Oskar's revived responsibility as Health Commissar was as before; the efficient running of the nation's hospitals. The familiar role nevertheless filled him with a apprehension.

He remained acutely aware that the janitor, a loyal Party Member, had discovered like thousands of our fellow Latvians that these so-called 'friends of the workers' were not to be trusted.

The janitor may not have been a likeable fellow, but the circumstances of his demise were sobering indeed. Now, Oskar's unexpected appointment was to be overseen by the same secret policeman, following hard upon the janitor's brutal end. Oskar's trepidation was further heightened when he observed the NKVD man holding a separate file marked *Meija, Oskar: Military Record,* because his service had been substantially against the Russians.

While Oskar had accepted his restoration with a mixture of relief and astonishment, he was also acutely aware that his authority, his every action and decision, would be under the NKVD man's constant scrutiny.

Time had appeared to stand still during his terrifying interview — in reality, it had been over in minutes. The relief that Mama and I felt at my father's safe return cannot be overstated. It also became true that, under that year-long Soviet regime, there was never a moment when any one of us felt safe or secure, nor a single night when we slept soundly.

From his now lofty but precarious position, Oskar could only stand by helplessly, observing the subjugation of his people, the demolition of their *esprit* and living standards, like a losing spectator at a one-sided football match.

Our spirit was broken. Before the Soviet invasion, Latvia had sustained as high a *per capita* living standard as any nation in Europe. By the end of that year, we were surely numbered amongst the most miserable of European nations.

*Displaced — A Modern Baltic Saga.*

Nevertheless, Oskar's term as Commissar brought tangible benefits and, to my parents' approbation, our new overlords at least maintained our national Opera, supporting both symphony concerts and the performing arts.

Oskar's NKVD watchman even displayed an occasional glimpse of humanity. And so it was, one early evening just before Christmas 1940, that Nadja and I called in at Oskar's office on our family's way to the opera, and found my father with his Soviet Comrades in a festive mood.

It remains a Latvian Christmas tradition that children are expected to recite a poem in order to receive their presents. That year my mother had taught me two versions; one in Latvian and another in Russian.

The conversation eventually turned to whether I had properly memorised my Christmas poem and, having replied in the affirmative, I was called upon to recite it.

Standing to attention, I dutifully spouted my rendition of the more difficult piece — several verses in the Russian language, about a boy entering a forest to choose a Christmas tree.

Both Russians seemed highly impressed, especially the NKVD fellow who (my father later told us) could barely read or write.

The NKVD man patted me on the head; "Juris, that was excellent! Your Russian is very good! How did you manage...?"

"Sir," I replied, "in order to learn, it is necessary to apply oneself."

My mother swelled with pride, the apparatchik beamed and my father giggled.

*Tens of thousands of Latvian, Lithuanian and Estonian men, women and children were compulsorily deported to remote regions of the Soviet Union — predominantly northern Kazakhstan and Siberia, where many perished in appalling circumstances. Pictured above are the conditions in a Siberian deportee village, showing the desolation during a spring thaw.*

The NKVD man chuckled and once more patted my head.

"Juris, you are absolutely correct."

Much relieved, we made our way to the National Opera House. We could all recall our family life before our nation's invasion — confident times, full of laughter and happiness.

Those days were gone, and the fear of betrayal, death or deportation lurked in every laneway, around every corner.

We were witness to our formerly proud and carefree national culture withering beneath the icy hand of totalitarian oppression. Even our closest friends could no longer be trusted.

At school, Stalinist dogma took precedence over all other learning. Our lives had descended into a dreadful hell inhabited by a myriad of demons.

In the event, our family did manage to survive our small nation's 'Year of Terror,' but in the meantime, more than 35,000 of our fellow Latvians were either murdered or simply disappeared.

*Riga's majestic Latvian National Opera House (Est. 1912) as it appears today.*

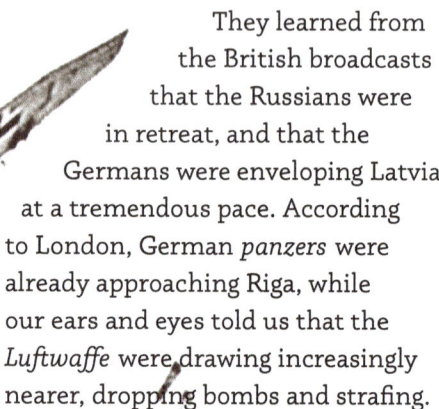

## 1.3  Nazi Invasion

Our Soviet terror ended abruptly in the summer of 1941, when Hitler's German forces took their turn to invade our nation. Because the Soviet occupiers had been roundly detested, it seemed at first that most Latvians rejoiced.

As a prelude to the Russians' exit, Oskar had received a directive from his Soviet masters that the Nazis were invading the motherland, and that he should prepare himself and his family to withdraw to safety in Russia, forthwith.

Meanwhile, the Soviet propaganda machine was in full swing, promulgating the false narrative that our brave Soviet fighters were holding their ground and resisting the Nazis at every turn.

My parents preferred to get their news from the BBC however, tuning in their wireless set at night, muffled under their bedclothes for fear that our apartment had been bugged.

They learned from the British broadcasts that the Russians were in retreat, and that the Germans were enveloping Latvia at a tremendous pace. According to London, German *panzers* were already approaching Riga, while our ears and eyes told us that the *Luftwaffe* were drawing increasingly nearer, dropping bombs and strafing.

I well remember one pleasant childish summer morning. My Papa was busily occupied in his home office, speaking importantly on the telephone. His desk was placed at right angles to the outside wall, his chair set back from the window.

My Mama was in the kitchen, producing the comforting sounds and smells of food preparation.

I was in the lounge room, playing with my toys. There were two large windows, and between these windows were our sofa, a tea table and some chairs. Outside we could hear the soporific droning of distant aircraft and otherwise, or to me at any rate, our home seemed comfortable and secure.

Suddenly, we heard the swelling sound of an airplane approaching. Then, as the noise grew to a scream, there was an accompanying burst of machine guns and instantly, our whole apartment lit up in a brilliant flash.

Whether by obscure instinct or as part of some game, I was at that moment in the act of performing a spectacular handstand on the sofa when, with an almighty bang-crash, our lounge room windows imploded.

In that same instant, Oskar's office window also blew in and everything on his desk was cleared, including his heavy telephone.

Glass, pens, paper and shattered debris from all three windows were scattered everywhere, but thankfully, we three were completely unscathed.

A German bomb had exploded close to our apartment, presumably aimed at some opportunistic target in our street, and had detonated on the roof of the building opposite.

In the aftermath, my frantic parents rushed towards me and were overjoyed to see me standing unharmed by the sofa. I found myself simultaneously hugged, kissed, inspected and physically tested, all over.

I showed them how I had been standing on my head when the massive flash-bang had come. They were astonished to see sharp shards of glass and other debris scattered on the floor where seconds earlier I might have stood, evidently saved by my acrobatic manoeuvres — an incredible escape.

Within hours, German tanks were roaring across Riga's bridges, taking up position on our side of the Daugava, securing the river's crossings and their access for the following infantry. The Russians were defeated. Riga had been 'liberated' and we were physically intact.

Although he spoke German perfectly, Oskar was neither a Nazi nor a Nazi sympathiser. For the sake of our survival however, he preferred German rule as the lesser of two evils. Fortunately for us, the Nazis likewise recognised Oskar's bureaucratic talents and he was again retained as our nation's Health administrator. They appointed him to the Latvian Home Guard with the rank of Major.

Under German occupation, for our family at least, life became immediately more tolerable. We soon realsied however that our relief was to be short-lived, when it became clear that Latvia's 'liberation' was in fact a Nazi subjugation. The Nazis, like the Soviets, demanded civil obedience by instilling fear, their occupational policies involving a package of threatened forced labour, executions, deportations and death, with particular emphasis on Bolshevik sympathisers and the defenceless Jewish population.

With that growing realisation, my young mind became increasingly beset by storms of irreconcilable moral contradictions, the difference between good and evil having been already engraved into my thinking by an uncompromising Lutheran upbringing.

It dawned on me that no-one had satisfactorily explained why the Soviets' random executions had been acceptable, or why the 'friends of the workers' had deported thousands of ordinary families to Siberia. Likewise, why the Nazis were now rounding up all the Jews of Latvia — over 70,000 men, women and children — and like the Soviets, deporting them to mass executions or death-camps.

Our neighbours the Ringelsteins had been elderly, in their seventies — how could they possibly have harmed anyone? Neither could my mother explain why the Nazis had been moved to murder my Uncle Nicolai.

Nevertheless, despite our misgivings, life under Nazi rule seemed steady enough. As a non-Jewish child living in Riga, there seemed no obvious presence of war, and our home-life was what I might have imagined as normal.

My education continued. Mother began my piano lessons when I turned

*Displaced – A Modern Baltic Saga.*

six, having first had a music teacher assess my aptitude and conclude that I was "musically gifted."

My formal education began at about the same time. Mother would escort me to school in the morning and collect me in the afternoon. At home, after a light meal, she would make sure I practiced the piano. Sometimes she would stand behind me as I played, tapping me on the shoulder with a rolled-up newspaper if I made a mistake. "Play those bars three times again, please Juris," she would say.

When music practice was over it was time for homework and I would finish at around six. Later, my father would return from work and we would share a family meal. These were conversational occasions when I might be asked to relate what I had learned at school that day, as well as any new stories I might have.

After dinner I would sprawl comfortably on our settee and read. The English children's writer AA Milne was a favourite and I eventually launched into more complex works such as Mark Twain's Tom Sawyer, and Charles Dickens' David Copperfield.

In 1940, my love of Opera was awakened when my parents took me to a performance of Tosca. I have been an opera-lover ever since. I also recall summer vacations when Mama and I would stay in a country house outside Riga, and I would play soccer with the local farm boys.

Eventually however, the tide of war began to turn once more, and the Red Army began storming back towards us.

As a nine-year-old, I vividly remember that late August evening in 1944, the perturbation in my father's demeanour when he arrived home from work. He called Mama and me to sit with him in our cosy living room.

"We must go," Papa announced, in earnest, downcast tones. "The Soviets are coming back. The Red Army are advancing directly towards us,"

"They will doubtless be aiming to sieze Riga again and the Germans are in full retreat. We have no choice but to leave here now, as quickly as we can," he continued. "We can take only one suitcase each."

Naturally, my Papa's words brought a deluge of tears from Mama. Gripped by my mother's emotion and the urgent

*Žanis Lipke (1900-87) was one heroic example of the many Latvians who were appalled at the brutal excesses of Nazi occupation. He had been a dock worker in Riga when Germany seized Latvia in 1941. Witnessing the increasing Nazi persecution of Jews, he decided to risk his life by helping the city's Jewish population. He found employment at the Luftwaffe warehouses near the Central Market, where part of his job was to drive workers from the Jewish ghetto to the warehouses and back. He used this routine to conceal some of his passengers, so that they did not return to the ghetto and instead went to Lipke's home, where he had constructed a secret bunker to hide them. In total, Lipke and his helpers saved more than 50 Jewish lives. After the war, under Soviet occupation, Lipke was repeatedly interrogated by the NKVD as to where he had hidden all the gold and diamonds, which they believed he must surely have received as payment from the Jews he had saved. The Soviets had apparently found it impossible to believe that anyone would act as he had without a pecuniary motive.*

*The Latvia we left behind remains one of the most pristine places on Earth. Depicted is the peaceful Daugava River, for at least 4,000 years part of the principal overland trade route between the Baltic and Mediterranean regions.*

tone of my father's voice, struggling to hold back my own tears, I asked, "May I too have a suitcase, Papa?"

"You may Juris," my father replied, "but it must be the smallest one."

Then, holding his index finger to his lips. "And you must tell no one, do you hear? No one."

I had already learned that in times such as those, survival is the first consideration. I also have no doubt that, in deciding to escape in the direction of Nazi Germany, Oskar made the correct decision. There would have been literally no future for us with the Soviets.

Oskar realised that ending our war in rural Germany was probably our best chance of making a new life under more enlightened, Western circumstances.

Hearing my father's words, with all the bravado a young boy nearing ten could muster, I raised myself to my full height, clicking my heels in my most formal *kratzfus* fashion. With my hand resting on Nadja's shoulder, I declared, "Papa, we trust you. We will follow you wherever you lead. We will tell no one."

Papa embraced us. Mama shed bitter tears, like so many of her generation, at the loss of her home and possessions — of the countless memories woven into the fabric of our lives; of all that my parents had acquired and treasured.

We must leave that all behind us now, embarking on a dangerous journey towards an uncertain future, hoping beyond hope that we may eventually find somewhere secure and welcoming, to begin our lives anew.

That day was the beginning of a long and perilous odyssey to a different world; a journey I can never forget.

Any small excitement I may have felt was clouded with apprehension.

Yes, I reasoned, there would doubtless be many fascinating experiences — new people, villages, cities, languages — a true-life adventure.

But deep within me lurked a gut-wrenching sense of trepidation; an instinctive sensation of mixed dread, uncertainty and loss. And through it all, a hollow, stomach-churning grief at leaving behind the only place on earth I had ever called home.

The 1941 German occupation of Latvia brought with it immediate implementation of Nazi Party policy to rid Germany and its occupied lands of *Untermenschen* (sub-humans), the Nazi term for 'inferior' races, meaning principally Jews, Gypsies and Slavs, as well as any other individuals or groups whose works, conditions or opinions were disapproved of by Hitler.

As a result of this policy, in early December 1941, around 25,000 Jewish men, women, and children were murdered, on or soon after their forced march to the Rumbula Forest, just 12 kilometres from the heart of Riga.

Huge mass graves had been dug in preparation by 800 Russian prisoners of war. The shooting massacres were carried out, under direct orders from Himmler, by the SS *Einsatzgruppe A*, with the help of local collaborators and Latvian auxiliaries.

24,000 of the murder victims were Latvian Jews from the Riga Ghetto, and 1,000 more were German Jews who had been transported to the site by train.

Pictured above, at the Rumbula Forest site near Riga, is the modern-day public monument to this eternally shameful, horrific event.

## 1.4 What We Knew

We might well ask, looking back after some 80 years, to what extent was Nazi Germany's 1941 invasion of our nation a welcome reprieve from Soviet Russia's brutal oppression?

Under new German administration, the ethnic classification of our nation's population, and how quickly that process transmuted into violence, removes any suggestion that Germany's 1941 'liberation' of Latvia was anything other than a Nazi subjugation — along with everything which that entailed.

To what extent then, was Nazism resisted? Even a cursory investigation of the Holocaust in Latvia reveals beyond any doubt that most urban Latvians had some knowledge of the murder of Latvian Jews, and worse, that many were active participants.

Of course, it is easy in hindsight to suggest that Latvians might have done more to prevent the abrogation of more than a thousand years of mostly tolerant history, but the fact remains that, with their world at war, the people of Latvia found themselves very small players within a very large conflict.

In any event, Latvia's recent political past had been especially complex, wedged as our small nation was between the rise and catastrophic collision of two massive, expansionist and ideologically opposed foes.

In addition, Latvians had maintained age-old cultural and blood ties with both Germany and Russia, to the extent that old alliances and enmities could easily be merged, and to some extent transposed.

Living in Nazi-occupied Latvia required, indeed demanded under threat of death, the obedience and, to some psychological degree, the acquiescence of our native population, most of whom fell into one or more of the following categories.

First, there were vengeful Latvians determined to take up arms against the Russians who had terrorised our nation during 1940-41. Second, there were those hoping to keep a low profile; staying out of the Nazi military forces and work brigades. And lastly, there were pragmatists such as my father Oskar, who believed that by working with the Germans, Latvians would eventually be able to reclaim the Nation State the Soviets had dismantled.

In the end however, the war news for Germany deteriorated and survival became our most pressing concern. We were left with very few options.

As the fighting drew nearer, my parents could see no future for either themselves or me under a return of communist oppression. We chose to make our escape towards Germany, being the only destination that still seemed realistically open to us.

Today, with both Nazi Germany and the USSR having passed into history, Latvia is again an Independent Republic, proudly a Member of the European Union. Every Latvian who lived as an adult through those dreadful times will have likely passed away.

It therefore seems appropriate to, at long last, reflect upon the state of our emerging European nation — to choose which aspects of our dreadful wartime experiences we should accept as part of our national legacy, and which to discard as incongruous, un-Latvian aberrations.

*Displaced — A Modern Baltic Saga.*

# 2

PART TWO

# 2
# Taking Flight.

*The Latvian Division of Conscripts resisting the Red Army advance near Riga.*

## 2.1 Goodbye to Riga

In September 1944 the Red Army was pursuing a vengeful return into Latvia, directly towards Riga. We had no option but to flee the Soviet menace.

In anticipation, my father had earlier arranged for a truck to be sent ahead to Germany with our household possessions, although perhaps not surprisingly, we saw neither truck nor household goods ever again.

Oskar's plan was to leave Riga in our compact four-seat Adler sedan, and drive the 250 km to the Latvian seaport of Liepaja. From there we hoped to somehow escape by sea to Germany.

We loaded up before the break of dawn; suitcases, blankets, food hampers and a few personal items, and made our way out of the capital. Fortunately, the streets were deserted and, in silent reflection, we crossed the River Daugava without incident.

The Soviets were pressing from the south east, so we followed the coastal road, west from Riga, along a route that skirted the former recreational preserve of Riga's elite. We soon discovered that the Red Army was close by, clashing fiercely with the Latvian Division of Conscripts situated mostly to our north and west.

We must have made an odd early morning sight, my father in the uniform of a Latvian military officer, picking his way in a civilian vehicle through an active battle zone, with a lovely young woman and a frightened young boy.

All around us, explosions popped, banged and whistled, shells detonated and machine guns stuttered — we were in the middle of a furious battle.

We saw few other fleeing refugees as we manoeuvred through an obstacle course of burnt-out and burning buildings and military vehicles, strewn with the bodies of dead soldiers. It felt like trying to outrun a wildfire with both sides of the highway ablaze.

Barely beyond Riga's urban limits, our progress was completely halted near Jurmala. Dug-in Latvian militia were being charged repeatedly by waves of Red Army soldiers, who in turn were being efficiently mowed down by lomg, vicious bursts from the Latvians' Spandau machine-guns.

This was the first time I had witnessed the true horror of war. Eventually, with their casualties piling up, all enthusiasm drained out of the Soviets' repeated charges. The only Russian we could see left standing, hands held high, was a weeping and clearly traumatised female.

*Pictured is the 1938 Adler sedan, similar to that which carried us and our limited possessions in our escape from Riga. Adler was a German manufacturer of light vehicles from 1900 until 1957.*

*Displaced — A Modern Baltic Saga.*

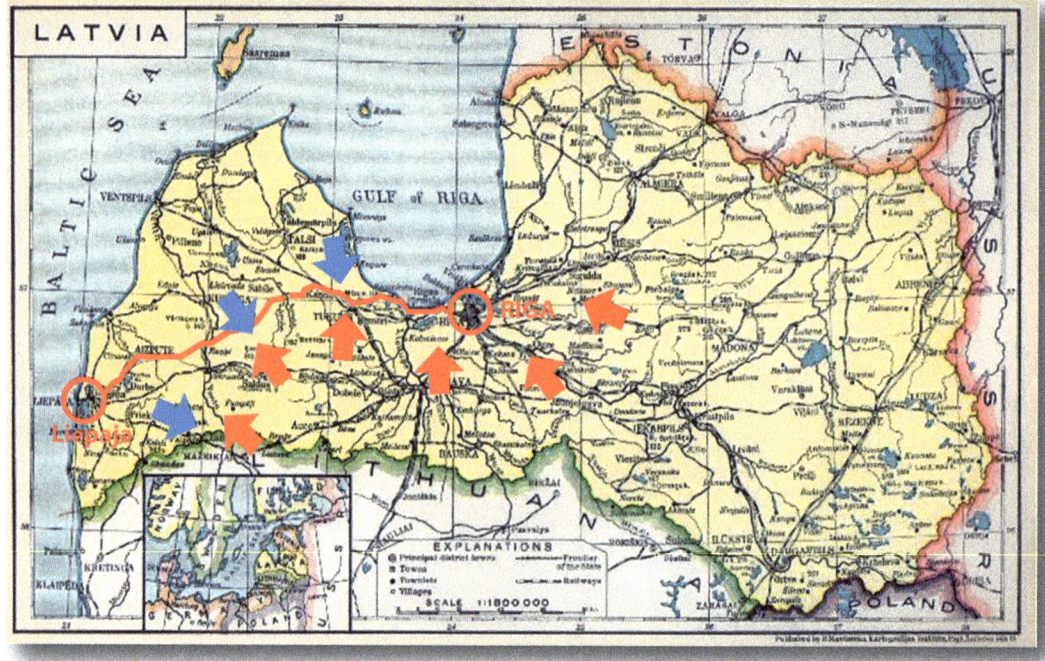

*The red line traces the approximate path of our perilous route from Riga to Liepaja, with the Red Army pressing from the South and East.*

Nadja prevailed upon the Latvian soldiers to spare the woman's life. She escorted her away and helped her clean up, before we were again able to proceed.

Our drive to Liepaja was beset by all of the terror and confusion one might expect from a headlong flight through a battle zone. At one point, for example, we emerged from woodland to be confronted by a Red Army patrol, who seemed every bit as surprised as we were. Oskar hurled the Adler into a hasty U-turn and we managed to disappear safely again, back the way we had come, without a shot being fired.

The direct route to Liepaja is not especially long, but for us there were many cautious detours. We travelled by back roads, spending at least one night sleeping on straw in a farmer's barn.

Petrol in wartime was of course virtually impossible to obtain, and we were acutely aware that the Adler would need refuelling if we were to make it all the way into Germany.

Nevertheless, for this wild, initial leg of our journey, our small sedan performed reliably well. At one point we struck an obstacle beneath the engine with a tremendous bang — apparently no real harm done.

Looking back, I realise it was truly miraculous that we made it unscathed to the seaport of Liepaja. Fortunately for our purposes, the local district was still in German hands.

## 2.2 A Narrow Passage

We found sanctuary at the Liepaja hospital. From there we ventured into town where we saw many refugees, mostly gathered in parks and open spaces. Amongst these were a family of farmers from the Jelgava region, with a 40-ton, wood-gas-powered truck.

The farmers were also hoping to escape the Red Army. Oskar, ever ready to seize an opportunity and mindful that fuel for our Adler was unavailable, made a bargain with the farmers where in return for official travel authorisation, they would tow our sedan behind their truck to an agreed destination in Germany.

Next, needing to create a credible travel justification for our truck and car combination, Oskar assembled a group of hospital employees including two doctors with their families, together with his Departmental Deputy. We would be 22 persons in all, with 3 babies.

Oskar was officially endorsed, as Director of Health, to issue the necessary travel documents. He listed the men in our party as doctors or orderlies, the women as nurses and, all together, our group as the essential staff of a hospital. These people with their personal belongings would travel in discomfort in the canvas covered back of the truck, while we would trail behind in our car.

A far greater challenge was how to get our vehicular convoy across the sea to Poland, from where we might conceivably motor into Germany.

The German freighter *Askaria* was one of several in the harbour. Oskar managed to engage the ship's Captain with an offer evidently too good to refuse — a box of medicinal alcohol from the hospital stores.

In this way, the farmers' truck, our car and all of our party would be officially embarked on the following day — ostensibly, essential cargo bound for Danzig in Poland.

That afternoon before our scheduled embarkation, the sounds of furious battle were discernibly closer. With German soldiers everywhere, Oskar decided it would be prudent to deliver our contraband under cover of darkness.

After placing the case of bottles in the trunk of the Adler, he was about to set off for his twilight delivery when I asked if I could come along. "Yes Juris you may come, but wear your warm jacket and hat."

I recall excitedly bidding my Mama a cheery farewell and jumping importantly into the Adler's front seat for our short drive to the harbour.

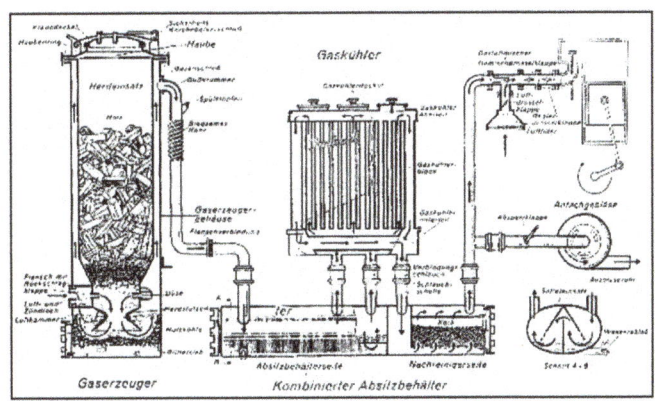

*A German wartime wood-gas powering arrangement for heavy vehicles. The main components in our truck were installed immediately behind the driver's cab and included a gas generator, a gas cooler and a precipitation tank. The system enabled a wide range of burnable fuel options including wood, charcoal, brown coal, peat and anthracite.*

The sentries waved us through and Oskar parked our sedan beside a sturdy brick building, adjacent to the Askaria's berth. Ordering me to remain quietly in the vehicle, he strode off and up the ship's gangway, his box of precious contraband under his arm.

I was happy to sit and watch the goings-on around the wharf. After some time I started to feel bored however, thinking that perhaps coming along had not been such a good idea, when abruptly, air-raid sirens began to wail, loud voices began shouting and nearby anti-aircraft guns started to fire.

Hurriedly, I leaped out of the vehicle and took shelter beneath it, from where I could watch the action. At first, the Russian bombs were falling harmlessly out to sea and I felt unthreatened. Then I saw a stick of bombs falling much closer, directly into the harbour and onto the adjacent wharf — they seemed to be coming straight for me.

Next thing, there was an almighty explosion, and suddenly, everything was eerily quiet once again.

Deafened, shaken, ears ringing, I crawled out from under the car, which appeared untouched, although covered in dust and debris. Oskar came running — he had seen everything from the bridge of the ship. Fortunately, the bomb had exploded on the far side of the sturdy brick building, which had protected both car and me.

"Juris," said Oskar, as we drove back to join Nadja at the hospital, "About that bomb. I don't think you should mention it to your mother." I promised to say as little as possible.

The following morning we loaded the truck, our car and passengers, ready for our sea voyage to Gdansk.

*Refugees boarding ships, Liepaja, October 1944. Most of the refugees' goods had to be left behind on the wharf — carts, furniture, domestic luggage and even farm animals. Oskar's powers of persuasion and innate intrepidity were the saving graces for our desperate party.*

With foresight, Oskar stashed an extra case of medicinal alcohol in the boot of the Adler, to serve as universal currency if needed. Finally, he clambered into the truck's rear to oversee the boarding of our passengers, who would huddle on cold wooden benches beneath the flimsy canvas. One of these, Dr Petkavicz, was coughing and evidently afflicted with tuberculosis.

"It sounds like the Doctor won't be making it," someone muttered.

"My friends," admonished Oskar, "Now is not the time for negativity or doubts — it's our time for action. Think of what this journey will bring to us. In any event, we won't stand a snowflake's chance in hell if we remain here in Liepaja. We will have real hope if we can just make it away. So please, keep your spirits up."

"Are we ready?" shouted Andris, cranking the engine, which chugged reluctantly into life. Oskar joined Nadja and me in the Adler and so resumed our epic flight, away from the Soviet menace, towards our ship, Gdansk and hopefully, to relative safety in Germany.

*The old town of Gdansk in Poland, reflected in the Motlawa river at sunrise.*

## 2.3 The Forge of Life

Despite the lurking presence of Russian submarines, our ship *Askaria* sailed without incident from Liepaja to Gdansk in Poland, her decks crowded with throngs of desperate refugees, plus our two vehicles.

From Gdansk we travelled on by road, preserving the Adler's precious fuel reserves by being towed behind the farmers' smoke-belching truck.

Within a few days, we reached the German-occupied town of Küstrin (Kostrzyn), only 90 km from Berlin.

That 1944 Kostrzyn Christmas is etched forever into my memory. The town's Catholic Church bells rang out to the glory of God and the birth of Jesus our Saviour, summoning the Christian flock and somewhat incongruously proclaiming; "Glory to God in the highest, peace on earth, goodwill towards men."

Snowflakes drifted down from heaven, blanketing the old town in a gleaming cloak of perfect white. How I loved the Christmas season!

Despite the Nazi occupation, Christmas for Christians in Poland was still a time of peace and goodwill. We dangled simple, home-made paper trinkets on the Tannenbaum, with red, white, gold and silver Yuletide motifs. On this occasion I especially enjoyed helping Nadja light the candles.

There was an antiquated piano in the church. I played my full repertoire of Christmas carols — Silent Night, Adeste Fideles, Away in a Manger, and my favourite, Little Drummer Boy.

*Küstrin (Kostrzyn) was to be utterly destroyed in the days after we left, in a desperate battle between the Wehrmacht and the advancing Red Army. The medieval town would eventually lie permanently in ruins, deserted and never to be rebuilt, when eventually the fighting moved on.*

For a brief time, our fears were set aside. We exchanged warm hugs and modest gifts. The men *skålled* rounds of medicinal alcohol. What were the women doing? Was there coffee and food? Later, in the evening, Oskar managed to scrounge a bottle of VSOP Brandy, which was savoured by all as the finest French Cognac.

Eventually we loaded up again and resumed our race towards safety. The cold, with our Adler's engine not running, was one discomfort, but my enduring memory is of suffering, hour after hour, the pervasive miasma of the acrid fumes billowing back from that wood-burning truck. The vile, burnt-toast stench, day-after-day, sickened me to the extent that I have never since been able to stand the smell of toasting bread.

Soon afterwards, there occurred the most traumatic experience of my life. We had been making our way steadily westwards through Eastern Prussia and, despite signs of mounting German resistance, the Russians seemed always close behind us. We felt barely ahead of the fighting, acutely aware that falling into enemy hands would almost certainly mean a terrible fate, when our truck chugged to an unscheduled stop in a deserted village. It seemed there was a problem with the carburettor, and we also needed more wood for fuel.

Andris and some of the other men were examining the truck's engine, while others were finding and chopping up wooden items to burn.

It was a gloomy winter's afternoon, the darkening countryside gleaming white with patches of snow and ice. Our babies were bawling with hunger and Nadja had been supporting the mothers, without success. She decided to try begging milk from a village we had recently passed through, where we had seen some lights and activity.

She looked around for Oskar and, not finding him, was readying herself to walk back over a hill to the recently passed village, alone and across country.

I had been watching Nadja's efforts and, without reference to her, prepared myself to go along and protect her.

A year or so previously, my Papa had taught me to handle the rifle that we kept in the Adler, a Mauser Karabiner with a telescopic sight.

Under his watchful tutelage I had learned to aim and fire the accurate weapon reasonably well. Mama had been opposed to our shooting lessons, but fortunately, as it turned out, my Papa had persisted.

I had the rifle and ammunition with me and was waiting for Nadja when she emerged, warmly dressed, carrying a small, empty milk can.

I had on my warmest clothing, the rifle slung over my shoulder. She opened her mouth to speak, at first I assumed to order me back into the vehicle, but then changed her mind and smiled. "Very well, my gallant soldier, let us walk together."

I adored my petite, ladylike Mama and her cheerful demeanour. She had been well educated in Russia; conversant in four languages, as well as writing poetry in French. Apart from our native Latvian, she had schooled me in German and Russian, which I spoke quite well, and taught me to recite poetry in three languages. She delighted in music and opera and supervised my piano lessons to the point where I could read music and enjoyed playing. With the horrors and deprivations of war all around us, my dear Mama was my guardian angel — my mentor, my guide and inspiration.

We set off in the gathering dusk, the moon shining bright, the air still and cold. There were no signs or sounds of war; our way ahead seemed safe enough. We trod carefully, side-by-side along the frozen path and up a gentle slope — a stroll in the countryside.

I thought I heard an owl, lifted the flaps of my hat and instantly became aware of men's voices, Russian. They seemed strident, loud, confident, the sound coming from somewhere ahead.

*7.92mm Mauser rifle with Zeiss telescopic sight.*

I motioned Mama to stop and we both listened. The voices were swearing in the way that only soldiers can. They sounded a little drunk.

I glanced back along our path and realised we had come too far to turn back unseen. By now, I could make out three figures silhouetted against the white, directly in our path and coming our way. I pushed Mama into a ditch and threw myself in front of her. Squinting through the rifle's telescopic sight, I saw three armed men walking toward us. The one in front held a Russian submachine gun, its round magazine obvious. The others had rifles. The ditch was too shallow to conceal us; they would certainly see us when they eventually drew close. Deliberately, I cocked the weapon and peered through its crossed-hair sights.

"Oh no! No, Juris..." urged Mama. "Don't shoot!" She was tugging at my trouser leg. "Please Juris no, please!"

It was clear to me that there was little choice. The soldiers were on a path leading directly towards us. I took aim at the man with the submachine gun, his weapon dangling in front of him. I knew, from overhearing soldiers talking, to aim for his body.

I remembered to allow for distance. Feeling far from confident, I adjusted the sights to one hundred metres. I took careful aim and squeezed the trigger.

The submachine gun man grabbed at his hip and both he and his weapon disappeared, presumably falling back into cover on the far side of the track. The other two seemed to disappear too — most likely, I thought, into the ditch nearer to us. We could hear all three calling out, urgently, doubtless trying to decide where the shot had come from.

Trembling with fear and excitement, I hesitated, uncertain. Should we run? No, they would surely chase and shoot us down.

In the field nearby were piles of harvested farm produce — sugar-beet. I might be able to catch sight of the remaining Russians, I thought, if I could reach the far side of the nearest heap. Nadja was sobbing now, behind me, pleading in frantic whispers that we should flee.

Defying my Mama, I scrambled across to the nearest pile. A man's voice called out that he had seen my movement near the heaps. Hugging the frozen earth, I squirmed around my pile and, keeping low, peered out.

Yes, there they were. The nearest had his head up, looking out from under his hat. To my astonishment, sighting him through the rifle's crossed hairs, I could make out his features, staring wide-eyed and directly at me. I had the rifle cocked and ready. Trembling, I took aim at the pale face, steadily exhaled, and squeezed the trigger.

The rifle bucked and a black spot appeared beside the man's nose. His head slumped forward, but now the soldier next to him was shooting — his bullet barely missing me. I was showered with pieces of beet. Deliberately, I slid over to the second pile and keeping as low as I could, again cocked the weapon.

From my new position, I could clearly see the third Russian through my scope, squinting one-eyed over the sights of his rifle. He'd seen me.

He fired first, his bullet striking the beets again, this time very close to my head. Adjusting, I took careful aim and squeezed the trigger once again. The fellow fell back, the life gone out of him.

*The wretched misconduct of the Red Army, in its relentless advance through Europe and into Germany, is well documented.*

At this juncture, to my complete astonishment, the first Russian jumped up and staggered into full view.

Hands high above his head, the man began to frantically shout in German, "Don't shoot! Comrade! No shooting!" Hesitating, I saw he still had his submachine gun, placed on the ground at his feet.

"Juris, you have no option," a voice in my head told me, as I deliberately re-cocked the Mauser. "You must shoot — there's no way you can handle a grown man with that automatic weapon in his hands."

I took aim at the Russian's chest and fired again — he fell backwards and lay still. I scrambled back to Nadja, who had been struggling to rise from her frozen hiding place. She had twisted her ankle and seemed capable only of hobbling.

I supported my Mama around her waist. We were limping in haste, back along the track, when dim figures appeared before us in the gloom. Papa was leading an anxious search party, furtively calling out. They had heard the shooting. We shouted back, as loudly as we could.

I have thought back countless times during my life, to this horrific episode.

I have pondered too, those dreadful events of 1938, when I was only three years old, when two of the world's most terrible dictators — Stalin, General Secretary of the Russian Communist Party, and Hitler, Leader of Germany's National Socialists — conspired between them for Germany to envelop the entire nation of Poland, and for Russia to absorb Latvia, Estonia and Lithuania.

Machiavellian plotting on a gargantuan scale, utterly beyond the control of ordinary folk, irrevocably damaging, disrupting and ending millions of innocent lives.

As a child, just nine years of age, I had already witnessed more horror and suffering than many adults would see in their entire lifetimes.

Inadvertently, I had been exposed to the countless contradictions of war — acts of compassion juxtaposed upon scenes of wholesale slaughter; gleeful exhilaration in face of unspeakable horror. Violence, death and destruction, too. And everywhere, that inescapable, gut-wrenching sense of foreboding; of all-pervading, sleep-depriving terror.

And, in the midst of it all, that ultimate of incongruities — each side fervently praying to the same God of Love and Compassion, for victory.

I wonder what many people these days might make of the horrors we endured, here in our brave new world of political correctness; of the need for *trigger warnings* and *safe spaces*; and of the desperate, drastic actions that in those times and in those circumstances, we had little choice but to undertake.

*Displaced – A Modern Baltic Saga.*

# 3

PART THREE

3

Drittes Reich.

## 3.1 An End in Sight

The Berlin we entered during those early weeks of 1945 was a beleaguered relic of its former glory.

Prior to Hitler's rise and the 1933 political domination of his Nazi Party, the city had blossomed into one of Europe's most appealing and diverse metropolises.

Despite the punitive constraints imposed by the Treaty of Versailles following Germany's defeat in the 1914-18 War, Berlin had been regarded by many as Europe's leading centre of cultural sophistication — literature, music, art, theatre, architecture, science, engineering, film production and much more.

Now, at this closing phase of the war, the once-splendid epicentre of Hitler's Third Reich seemed as broken as his Nazi dream of global domination. His enemies were closing in and Germany's appalling armed aggression was drifting inexorably towards ignominious defeat.

And yet the widespread destruction of German cities was only beginning. Ignoring the obvious, Hitler refused to capitulate, evidently determined to vent his frustration on his own people for the dissolution of his insane ambitions. Anyone could see that his cause was lost, but surrender was not in the Führer's vocabulary. "Let the people suffer!" he seemed to be saying. "It is their weakness, not mine, that has brought this ruination upon us!"

Ironically, over the English Channel, stood an equally dogged Prime Minister Winston Churchill, an aristocratic fossil of the 'Rule Britannia' era. Most suspected that a descendant of the great Duke of Marlborough could never have tolerated the impertinence of Hitler, a mere former Corporal, attacking the mighty British Empire — preposterous!

In fairness, and in contravention of the Geneva Convention, Göring's *Luftwaffe* had been first to rain bombs upon civilian targets in London and other urban centres, all over Britain. More than 60,000 British people had perished during those early raids, a provocation that Churchill was evidently determined to avenge.

In 1941, Churchill had ordered Britain's Royal Air Force, led by the ruthless Air Commodore Sir Arthur 'Bomber' Harris, to begin targeting German civilians – equally in breach of the conventional 'Rules of War.'

Later, as the Allies made territorial advances, and technological progress extended the ranges of Allied bombers and their fighter escorts, German populations became ever more vulnerable to air attack. City after German city was heavily targeted.

Our humble Latvian convoy groaned and squeaked to a smoky standstill on the eastern outskirts of Germany's once great capital. Oskar clambered busily around the two vehicles, assessing our situation, puffing out clouds of vapour in the frosty air.

Eventually, addressing us all, he pronounced, "Dr Petkavicz's condition is clearly critical — we must find urgent medical attention. Therefore, my family and I will go ahead in the Adler to consult with my friend, the eminent physician, Dr Heinz Schrieffer."

To those who were to remain behind with the truck, he said, "Very early in the morning, those of you in the truck will travel with Andris, as unobtrusively as possible, around the city's outskirts.

"We will meet you again to the West, at a place that Andris and I have agreed.

"Andris, you and only you, are to deal with any challenges — your German is good enough to be taken for a local.

"Above all, you must avoid attention. Remain hidden as far as possible. Take it in turns to use that shovel if you must, there is privacy under the bridge."

For those sheltering beneath the truck's flimsy canvas, life had been becoming ever more nightmarish. This was further exacerbated by the frigid conditions and the constant tubercular coughing of Dr Petkavicz, erupting from his chest as regularly as the strike of a grave-digger's mattock.

Hardly surprisingly, cold, hungry, unwashed and miserable as our refugee companions were, crammed together on the truck's hard wooden benches with little food and few comforts, frequent bickering, complaining and squabbling had become the norm.

Even as Oskar started walking towards us, Mama and I could hear their rising babble of discontent.

Oskar turned and climbed back into the truck. "Now listen to me, you people," he growled unapologetically. "Each of you pleaded for a place on this journey. I never promised you first-class travel. I never promised you anything — just a place in a truck.

"Most of our countrymen would have given their right arms to be here with us. So please, no more of this nonsense."

Drawing the canvas flaps closed, Oskar jumped down and joined Mama and me in the Adler. Without so much as a backward glance, he started the engine and we motored smoothly away.

*Berlin had been a global leader in modern architecture. Pictured is the city's Shell Hause, strikingly advanced for 1930. Despite its international acclaim, Hitler strongly disapproved of the design, insulting the architect Fahrenkamp with "So, you're the man who committed the crime of the Shell Building!"*

## 3.2 A Welcome Respite

The Schleifers' home was on the outskirts of Berlin. Our brief drive to their village, free at last from the truck's choking fumes, was as pleasant as it was uneventful. We savoured the fresh, crisp winter air — relishing it with the relief that desert stragglers must feel in wetting their parched throats at an oasis.

At her door, Frau Hildegard Schliefler greeted us like long-lost family. The Doktor welcomed Nadja in the European way, three kisses to her cheeks, before embracing Oskar in a bear hug that expelled air audibly from his lungs. Finally, he shook my hand formally, declaring: "My goodness, Juris, how you have grown since I last saw you in Riga!"

I smiled proudly, rising to my full height. "*Danke, Herr Doktor*, I'm nearly up to my Mama's shoulder now."

Beaming, the Doktor turned again to Oskar, "My dear friend, how wonderful to see you all. You must all be exhausted from your journey. Be seated and we'll share some of my French Cognac — it's XO."

"French cognac — and Extra Old too!" exclaimed Oskar. "Danke, Heinz! You must have excellent connections!"

"I took the precaution of stocking up on cognac before the war, and have stored it here in our cellar. I expect it will prove an excellent investment, once these troubled times have subsided."

"It will be gold," said Oskar, well aware, as we had observed, of the value of alcohol as a trading commodity. His nose twitched as he swirled the amber fluid, inhaling and exhaling the fumes with a sound much like waves sweeping a sheltered beach.

"My good friend!" boomed the Doctor. "You must have quite a story!"
"Indeed we have," replied Oskar, rising to clink glasses with his friend. He gave a brief account of our travels, omitting the more horrific aspects.

They discussed the precarious condition of our poor Dr Petkavic, and Heinz made his recommendations.

The Schleifer's home was warm and made even more inviting by the tantalizing aroma of baking cake.

"Hildegard is preparing a coffee for us — *ersatz* unfortunately, but that's wartime for you."

"Ah, coffee — how wonderful, thank you Heinz!" exclaimed Nadja. "But what news is there of your sons?"

Instantly, a despondent silence fell. Nadja must have wished she could suck back her words. The grief-stricken face of our host told the story.

Choking back tears, Heinz replied, "We've heard nothing from our boys — almost two months, now. It's not like them at all, but we live in hope. Hope is all that lingers," he added sadly.

"Each day on the wireless they tell us how well the *Wehrmacht* are doing on all fronts. If it's true they're doing so well, I'd hate to see Berlin if they were doing badly. We civilians have no voice in the matter. We can only wait helplessly for each night's bombing, to see if our number comes up."

"In that regard, Oskar," Heinz continued, grimly. "Grey skies might have afforded us some brief respite, but I see there's not a cloud in sight tonight. Nowhere in the city will be safe. Why not stay here with us?"

"Thank you, Heinz, your kindness is most considerate," replied my father, "but we have nineteen helpless compatriots depending on our safe return — and I am their leader."

Heinz persisted, "My friend, at least rest safely here with your family for one night, in our village. Everywhere in the city streets will be deadly dangerous, as I'm sure you must be aware…"

As Heinz was speaking, Hildegard entered, pushing a trolley laden with her freshly made coffee and the beguiling centrepiece of her labours, a magnificent, oven-warm cherry cake.

My first experience of deprivation had been on our journey — weeks of anxious, close confinement between my parents on the front seat of our small sedan — trundling, squeaking behind a sour truckload of squabbling refugees, with its choking, all-pervasive, eye-watering, burned toast fumes, my belly constantly groaning with hunger.

Having subsisted for many weeks on the most meagre of rations, I was transfixed now by the sight of Hildegard's perfectly-formed cherry cake, a slice of which was surely about to enter my drooling mouth.

I must have arrived in heaven!

Hildegard regarded me fondly as I savoured the last lip-smacking morsel.

"Now Juris, your Mama tells me you've turned ten on this journey. So, we must sing for your birthday!

"Indeed, I made this cake especially for you. I'm sorry that we do not have a candle. But Juris, please remain seated, and everyone else, please stand."

The adults rose and sang in German, followed by three hearty cheers:

*"Congratulations to you,*
*congratulations to you,*
*congratulations to you, Juris,*
*congratulations to you!"*

I was truly in my element — the centre of attention, my deprived belly full of cherry cake, and every adult in the room regarding me with affection.

"Juris, seeing I have done my best for you," Hildegard continued, "Nadja tells me you play the piano beautifully..."

"Oh, but Frau Schliefler. I am just learning..." I responded coyly, earnestly hoping to deflect her enthusiasm. Every adult, I knew well, suffered the performances of learner-musicians with varying degrees of displeasure.

My strategy failed. Oskar, buoyed with cognac, loudly reassured Hildegard that I was most talented for my age.

"Oh, do play for our hosts Juris, and for your Mama and Papa also, please."

There could be no escape.

Reluctantly, I crossed to the piano and perched myself tensely on the black stool, my back straight as a birch.

I composed myself and began the slow, deliberate notes of Beethoven's *Moonlight Sonata No. 2 in C-Sharp minor.*

For theatrical effect, as I'd seen various performing concert pianists do in Riga, I flicked my blonde hair from time to time, adding dramatic emphasis to the familiar melody.

I played with such heartfelt empathy that the haunting melancholy of my performance extracted every last morsel of merriment from the occasion.

By the time my recital ended, the cheerful atmosphere in our hosts' velvet-curtained *willkommen* 'welcome' room had turned deeply sombre, the mothers' faces streaming with tears.

Perhaps Hildegard could see her missing sons in me, playing that same melody, which perhaps they too had learnt as boys and practised on that same piano, in that very room.

I knew also that my Mama, and Papa too, would be thinking of our Riga home, now lost to us forever.

A chorus of appreciation burst from my audience. Oskar, sensing the mood, stood up and placed his arm around my shoulders.

"Bravo Juris! Bravo my son, very well done." Compliments from my father were few and greatly treasured.

I beamed with pride and pleasure — one of those indelible moments in a young boy's memory.

*Not too far from where we sang and celebrated, the Red Army were continuing their advance as Berlin's defences collapsed. Here we see a Russian T-34 tank passing by the bodies of dead German soldiers, lying in their ruined positions.*

*Boy-musician Juris, entertaining friends and family.*

Oskar then settled himself jauntily at the keyboard. He threw out his coattails and began playing well-known popular tunes, singing along with gusto in his slightly tone-deaf manner, boisterously entreating us all to join in.

In future years and in many respects, the entertainer in me would come to emulate my father. In those days, my childish vocal chords still emitted the treble tones of a choirboy. Nevertheless, I joined my father with enthusiasm and soon our tears were dried away; loud voices, good cheer and laughter once more filling the room.

In a matter of minutes however, our joyous mood was again extinguished, this time by the distant, ominous wailing of sirens.

Oskar stopped playing, his body tensed with urgency. This was no time to abandon his charges!

Abruptly, he rose from the piano and goodbyes were hastily exchanged.

"A thousand thanks, Hildegard and Heinz, for your wonderful hospitality. You have been so very kind. We hope we can reciprocate when these dark days are over. May God bless you, and bring your sons home safely!"

"May God bless you too, and your fellow travellers," replied Heinz. "And be careful Oskar, tonight in the city. The bombing is so very fierce. It's like Russian Roulette to say the least, and believe me, there is more than one live bullet in those six chambers."

The women hugged, clinging together in silent, tearful embrace.

Oskar was already seated in the vehicle, his hands tightly gripping the steering wheel, anxious to be away.

At last, final farewells exchanged, we three purred away in our Adler. Mother and I continued to wave until our kind and generous friends were entirely lost to our sight.

*By late 1944, operating from bases all over the United Kingdom, Royal Air Force ground crews were refueling and arming scores of ominous, dark-painted Avro Lancaster bombers, in preparation for further, terrifying night bombing raids over German cities.*

## 3.3  Fiery Retribution

A still, clear darkness was settling over Berlin. Bright stars were beginning to twinkle in the deepening blue sky.

A short drive and then more waving — this time, German uniforms ordering us to halt. My father stepped out of the Adler and a Corporal demanded papers, which Oskar presented.

Mama and I listened in silent apprehension to my father's exchange with the Corporal, a young lad who seemed not much older than some of the boys from my school.

In Riga, I had been taught to avoid soldiers, and here we were, foreigners on the soldiers' home soil, in a land where we were now the strangers.

Finally, "Now see here, Corporal!"

My Papa was raising his voice, impatiently. "This travel is authorised by me personally as a German Army Officer and Head of Health Department of Latvia. Do not delay us any further, or I will have you disciplined. Do you understand?"

Having previously experienced the behavioural unpredictability of soldiers under challenge, my whole body began to tremble, frozen in anticipation of the armed soldier's response.

*"Jawohl Herr Major!"* The young soldier clicked his heels in *kratzfus* fashion with a *Heil Hitler* salute. My brave Papa resumed his place at the wheel — I felt so proud of him.

We drove on, lights out, through silent, darkening streets. Increasingly we heard the thrumming drone of heavy bombers, high overhead, gathering like ravens to inflict fresh wounds upon the heart of their already vanquished foe.

I had experienced the sound of bombers before and had twice been physically bombed, but this time was the most vulnerable I had ever felt.

Soon, powerful shockwaves were shaking our car with gigantic, staccato thudding as the air crews disgorged their deadly cargoes onto the city's helpless civilians, cowering far beneath them.

Unlike soldiers, civilians have no surrender option. We felt naked, the exposed targets of a vengeful Churchill, determined to bring not just Hitler, but every German to their knees.

In fairness, considering these events in perspective, Germany had twice in just two decades been the instigator of the industrial-scale death and mayhem that only modern warfare can inflict. It seemed now that Churchill was determined his enemy would never again rise to wreak such havoc. Earlier, Germany's *Luftwaffe* had itself violated the conventions of war by bombing British civilians, and now Britain would reciprocate — every German a target for annihilation.

At this late stage of the war, Germany was retreating on all fronts. The war was surely almost over, and yet the Führer still refused to capitulate. And so the Allies continued to rain terror down on Germany, from skies that they largely controlled.

"These British were supposed to be the good guys," I had thought. "Surely, humanity's behaviour could hardly be any worse."

And yet, in a little more than six months, the Nazi State-sanctioned murder of millions of Jews, Gypsies, Slavs, political dissidents, homosexuals, disabled people and prisoners of war, would be exposed for all the world to see. Helpless victims, brutally exterminated by Nazi death squads. Unequivocal evidence that human beings were capable of acting even more reprehensibly — and had.

That night, despite the pressing dangers, Oskar remained steadfast in his determination to return to our refugees. On we drove, through deserted streets, under a starry sky.

*2,000 Berliners died in this single air raid, and 175,000 were made homeless. The intense bombing lasted until March 1945. By then, half the homes in Berlin had been ruined and an estimated 50,000 civilians had been killed. This number would have been much higher had it not been for the city's excellent bomb shelters.*

The beams of searchlights split the heavens, the whine of the Adler's gearbox interspersed with the violent thunder of serial detonations, shockwaves, flashes and bright fire storms rising from the city's defensive batteries.

It is impossible to adequately describe the sound and fury of such a bombardment. Like the immense power of a mighty waterfall, the explosions around us merged to an almost continuous roar. To us, so very much exposed, imminent oblivion seemed ever closer and more likely.

Terrified, I stared out, my teeth chattering, at the violent mayhem all around us. Light beams criss-crossed the darkness, sparks of anti-aircraft fire dotted the sky, the bright orange tracer streams, distant overhead flashes, and the occasional earthward death-arc of a blazing aircraft.

Worst of all, the thrumming of countless heavy bombers overhead, and the indescribable, terror-inducing succession of whistling, rippling bangs that shook and re-shook us to our core.

I thought of the people, more sensible than we were, cowering in relative safety within the city's many concrete shelters. For the first time in my life, I questioned Oskar's wisdom in driving us so relentlessly onwards.

"Please Papa, can't we take shelter?"

As if to lend emphasis, the sky began showering bright-hot shrapnel, heavy hailstones of metal fragments from the city's anti-aircraft barrage. I could feel my Mama's terror and was no longer capable of feigning bravery. My whole being trembled in my shock and fear, the air acrid with firestorm smoke and the reek of cordite.

"Stay calm! Both of you — be calm," urged Papa. "There is nowhere for us to hide. It's safer for us here, on the move, believe me." Even as he spoke, the sound of bombing began to subside.

The firing of the anti-aircraft batteries sporadically abated. In the relative quiet we could hear the crackling of flames and the roar of firestorms. Distant voices, shouting, calling out. And all around us, smoke, death and devastation.

Many buildings were gutted with bright flames. One ahead of us collapsed with a splintered roar, strewing debris across our path. Oskar braked heavily to a stop. Wide-eyed, we climbed out onto the cobbled street.

Rubble was almost entirely blocking our path ahead, except for a narrow passage with a lesser scattering of debris, a wrecked cart and a dead horse. Oskar attached the animal's traces to the Adler's bumper and we managed to drag the unfortunate creature aside. Nadja began clearing a path through the rubble where the dead horse had been.

I was helping Oskar when instantly we were both knocked over, deafened by a mighty bang, blinded by its brilliant flash. Our car seemed to jolt bodily up on one side before bouncing back again onto its four wheels.

Fresh bricks and mortar chunks were dropping all around us. Nadja had disappeared — nowhere to be seen. Like a ragdoll, she had been tossed by a delayed bomb, exploding so close it seemed, less than fifty metres away.

"Mama!" I screamed. Papa and I lurched toward where she had stood, dazed, stunned, our ears ringing, to find her. She was face down, unmoving.

"Mama, Mama," I called out, terrified of losing her. Kneeling beside her limp form, anxiety was gripping my chest so tightly I could barely breathe.

Oskar rushed forward with a water bottle and his handkerchief. Nadja was alive, semi-conscious, abrasions to her hands and face. Papa applied the wet cloth and gradually she came back.

"Where am I? What happened?"

"Where is Juris?"

I reassured her, "Here Mama, I am here," feeling the same sense of relief she must have felt at the sound of her only child's voice. Tenderly, we lifted and carried her to the car.

I was preparing to climb in next to her when I glanced towards where the delayed explosion had occurred.

Fresh bright flames and thick smoke were tearing upwards through a newly shattered building. In the glowing firelight, I noticed a human-like bundle, motionless on the road.

Hurrying towards the still shape, I stopped in horrified realisation that the unmoving mass was the pulverised, gore-oozing remains of a dead human.

Appalled, I tore my gaze away and lifted my eyes upwards, toward the blazing, devastated structure.

*Berlin burning.*

Clearly visible in the orange half-light were the shattered interiors of wrecked apartments, a piano half-hanging from an upstairs floor — an image I can never forget.

Nadja had recovered somewhat and was weakly urging me back to the Adler. I turned and was instantly transfixed by the sight of two upright figures, struggling against a lurid black-and-orange backdrop of flame, smoke and wreckage.

Unconscious of the danger, I hurried towards the pair — a small girl screeching in distress as she and her mother struggled to walk, glued by their shoes to the molten surface.

In peaceful times back in Riga, my Mama had taken me to an exhibition of paintings by the Norwegian artist Munch. I had been transfixed by his work 'The Scream' — an image that had shocked me deeply. The artist seemed to have captured the horror of a human about to be engulfed in an inferno.

That night in Berlin, this small, traumatised girl reminded me of that horrific painting — an image that has haunted my nightmares ever since.

Somehow, I managed to half carry, half drag the howling child to cooler, firmer ground, while Oskar rushed forward for the woman.

We extinguished their smouldering garments with our gloved hands. The girl's hat was still smoking — I pulled it from her head. In the flickering firelight I could make out raw patches of missing skin and hair, her face deeply scorched. She was clutching a doll, its hair likewise partly scorched away, showing bright patches of ceramic skull.

Oskar helped the pair to our vehicle.

'The Scream' — the popular name of the famous 1893 painting by Norwegian expressionist Edvard Munch. The work is the closest expression of the horror that Juris and his family experienced in the bombing of Berlin.

Nadja, herself only barely recovered, was tenderly applying what remained of our water. Weeping, sobbing "Danke... Danke!" A scene of compassion I can never forget.

"Can we drive you somewhere?"

"Oh, thank you, yes thank you!" cried the woman. "Please, would you take us to the home of my parents?"

The woman's name was Erika, her five-year old, Gisela. "It's not very far, assuming we can get through..."

"Juris, you will have to ride on the running board," directed my father.

I clung like a hero to the outside of the vehicle. Oskar started the engine and we moved cautiously ahead.

Feeling heroic yes, but also somehow inadequate, incapable of easing Gisela's wailing agony, or mending the scars she would surely carry throughout her life.

Oskar threaded our way through the smoke-obscured, rubble-strewn streets, steering under Erika's direction.

A short drive and once again we were being waved down. This time by a group of boisterous revellers, apparently celebrating their survival of yet another death-dealing onslaught.

Nadja requested more fresh water, which was brought and gently applied. Oskar accepted the rowdy, insistent group's offer of Schnapps.

Half a salami and several alcoholic refreshments later, we eventually arrived at Erika's parents' home, to yet more hospitality. It was past midnight before we could politely extract ourselves and continue towards our rendezvous.

We found our anxious Latvians without much difficulty, about an hour later. The truck was not far from where Oskar had expected it to be, its canvas cover white-frosted and steaming. An insipid pink and orange dawn was just beginning to tinge the smoke-obscured eastern horizon.

A brief reunion, and Andris was again cranking the wood gas engine into smoky action. Our grumbling, creaky caravan was soon trundling forward — this time, thank goodness, towards our ultimate destinations.

I dozed on my Mama's soft and gentle shoulder, blanket-wrapped and bone-weary on our cramped front seat, utterly spent from the night's exertions.

Trailing along for that final time, the familiar, choking, burnt toast stench once more assailed our nostrils. This time however, after the extreme horror and stress of our recent experiences, the discomfort of the truck's acrid fumes seemed a trivial distraction — one that no longer bothered me.

*Adolf Hitler was perhaps driven psychologically to wage war in 1939 — only two decades after the 1914-18 Great War had destroyed the lives of millions. By 1945, in just the sixth year of his vaunted 'Thousand Year Reich', more than five million of his fellow Germans had lost their lives and much of Europe lay in ruin. Pictured here in 1945 during the war's last days, in possibly his final public appearance, Hitler is seen awarding medals to school-age members of the Volkssturm or Hitler Youth — some of the futile, last-ditch defenders of his Nazi dream.*

## 3.4 Final Skirmish

By the Spring of 1945 the land battles were nearing their climax.

The Soviet, American and British armies were forcing their way into Germany from every direction. Berlin was their obvious military objective and, not that we were aware of it, a powerful Red Army encirclement of Hitler's capital was already well underway.

Having previously sampled Soviet Russia's "Year of Terror," Oskar's primary intention throughout had been to remove us as far as possible from territories likely to be occupied by the Soviets, and thus subject to totalitarian oppression.

His aim had been achieved, as near as we could have expected him to make it. For the most part, and to a large extent miraculously, he had led our desperate band to a place of relative safety. His promise now fulfilled, it was time for us to go our separate ways and soon afterwards, our group dispersed.

We were all much relieved to have delivered the critically ill Dr Petkavicz, our journey's only physical casualty, to a sanatorium. Sadly, we later learned that he had succumbed to his disease.

On our own at last, my parents and I found rural refuge in Lower Saxony — a mostly untouched western German province that Oskar reasoned would likely be overrun by British or American forces. These, we understood, would be approaching us from the south-west.

*In the spring of 1945, an exhausted and dispirited Waffen-SS rifleman, pictured in the general vicinity of Wellendorf. At this (for him) hopeless stage, German units in the region were surrounded, cut off from their main forces and running critically short of supplies.*

```
12th (10th Battalion The Green Howar
Commanding Officer : Lt Col K. T. Dar
18th April 1945
Place: Nienwohlde
0630 - Bn moved by march route to KA
0830 - Bn HQ established.  German ci
many barns which had been fired in ac
0945 - Approx 300 enemy reported in
pocket.  Bn prepared to move to WELL
1200 - Orders received for whole Bn
The plan was to move across the Sout
ATK guns was in support.
1415 - Bn moved off with B Coy leadi
there was no apparent sign of enemy
sition on high ground South of WELLE
at 016873.  B Coy then cleared the v
1530 - WELLENDORF completely cleared
BATENSEN 0388, and A Coy to NATELN 0
and B Echelon formed a tight localit
Airlanding Anti-Tank Battery arrived
troop with B Coy and Bn HQ.  5 priso
No incidents occurred during the nig
19th April 1945
```

We rented an upstairs hotel room in Wellendorf, a village about 220 km west of Berlin. Wellendorf had until that time been spared the palpable shocks of war, but our senses told us that land and air battles were drawing inexorably nearer — cause for continuing anxiety.

I well remember that final morning, when a truckload of German soldiers, dishevelled, shivering, exhausted and dispirited, pulled up on the roadway outside our accommodation. Rousing our landlady by knocking, they respectfully requested boiling water to make tea, and were rudely refused.

Nadja was aghast at this heartless rejection and, in her usual fashion, made sure that the needs of the weary men were accommodated.

Gratefully, the dispirited looking soldiers drove off in the direction of a nearby wooded hill, which we could see from our upstairs window.

Later that day, watching from our window, we witnessed a military action on that hill, where presumably those same weary soldiers were engaged and quickly rounded up by elements of the 12th Battalion of the British Parachute Regiment — the *Red Berets*.

And so it was that by way of good fortune, Nadja's compassion and Oskar's adroit leadership, we found ourselves physically unscathed in what was to become Germany's 'British Sector.'

*The regimental insignia of the British 12th Parachute Battalion.*

```
ate Battalion.



3.

our was set to work on burying the dead cattle in
 days previously.

LENDORF 9087 attempting to escape from UELZEN
s A Coy and elements of HQ Coy.

WELLENDORF, 13 Para Bn taking over KAHLSTORF.
of WALLENDORF and approach from the East.  1 Tp of

ORF could be clearly seen from Klei Pretzier and
ecided to approach direct.  B Coy moved into po-
oint 81, 0186, then C Coy moved astride main road
 found no enemy.

tablished rear cross roads.  C Coy moved out to
 took up position on ridge at 016873 and Bn HQ
e crossroads.  A second troop of ATK guns from 6
p was deployed forward with ATK
aken in the forward areas.  1
```

*An extract of Wellendorf entries from the Regimental Diary of the British 12th Parachute Battalion, 18 March 1945*

*Displaced — A Modern Baltic Saga.*

In later years I brought my two sons with their mother Rhys to Wellendorf and showed them where that final battle had taken place.

Until then I had been unaware that elements of the Soviet Army, in their encircling 'Battle of Berlin,' had reached only a few kilometres to the East. That had indeed been a narrow escape — too narrow for us, perhaps.

Not long after the Wellendorf action, Hitler removed himself by taking his own life, and Germany's unconditional surrender was signed in May 1945.

The world's most appalling conflict was over, too late to save the tens of millions who lost their lives, loved ones, livelihoods, health, homes — and some of us, our entire nations.

The cruel ambition of tyrants had left an indelible mark on our small country. After the war, it was estimated that, as a consequence of those three successive invasions, ignoring the many thousands who had earlier fled and found refuge abroad, around 150,000 Latvians died or disappeared from deportation, executions or military action. This included an estimated 70,000 Latvian Jews and, in addition, 20,000 Central and Eastern European Jews who had been transported in and murdered upon our soil.

We had indeed been fortunate. The Wellendorf action we witnessed was our final wartime incident.

Immediately after that brief clash, we were summarily ejected from our hotel and relegated to a garden shed by a Company Commander of the Red Berets. He was a perhaps unsurprisingly belligerent fellow who threatened to shoot my father.

Eventually we were told by an equally disparaging and bombastic sergeant, that we could return to our hotel room. We took their insults in our stride.

Not long afterwards, on a balmy, spring afternoon with barely a hint of breeze, Nadja, Oskar and I strolled across the road and up to a small hill, from where we could view the peaceful countryside.

At long last, we felt safe and free. The gross stupidity of war, the blood, the streets and meadows strewn with dead bodies, seemed to be over. The killing, the destruction, the all-pervasive dread — finally, at long last, all around us seemed quiet and serene.

Not a word was spoken. Together, we stood in silence, holding hands, looking, lost in our thoughts. At last, my mother spoke.

"Thank God!" she murmured, quietly. "We survived!"

*The agelessly tranquil farmland near Wellendorf, as it appears today.*

*For us, the tranquillity of Lower Saxony countryside was the perfect antithesis to the horrors of war.*

*Displaced — A Modern Baltic Saga.*

PART FOUR

4

Self Reparation.

## 4.1 Finding Our Feet

We left Wellendorf in the Spring of 1945 and found sanctuary in the rural hamlet of Hohnsen, still in Lower Saxony, near the medieval market town of Hameln, on the River Wesery.

*Hohnsen today. Ref: Google Earth 2021.*

Hameln is best known for its legend of the Pied Piper, a story based on a real incident that occurred in the 13th century, although somewhat less sensationally than the popular myth.

With his usual resourcefulness, Oskar established a transport business in Hohnsen and our lives once more assumed a semblance of normality. He had managed to recover several abandoned military trucks from the surrounding woods; vehicles that could be conveniently recovered, repainted and adapted for civilian use. He stashed these in the barn of a local farmer and began a commercial enterprise that was soon operating for profit.

Our cottage in Hohnsen is still there, more-or-less at the centre of the village, adjacent to the church.

For several years I attended the famous Schiller-Gymnasium school in Hameln, about 12 kms away. The school was ancient, founded in 1133. It had maintained a significant status in the region, having for centuries served a reputational as well as educational function for the town and its region. For example, in 1910 the then 'grammar school' was educating over 600 students, half from outside Germany. The institution was renamed the 'Schiller-Gymnasium' in 1947, during the time I was a pupil there.

Germany's bureaucracy was in disarray after the war, so our teachers were mostly older fellows who emerged from retirement. They did an excellent job. Their curriculum covered a wide range of subjects from Mathematics to Art, and between lessons I played chess with my friends.

We were taught so well that when my Mama and I eventually settled in South Australia, I sat for the 1951 State's Intermediate Exams and passed in every subject, including English.

Each school day, I would pedal my battered old pushbike a short distance from our home, whatever the weather, to catch a train to Hameln. My beloved bicycle was a symphony of postwar improvisation. For example, amongst other modifications, I replaced the useless front tyre with a circle of rubber hose that I joined with wire. Obviously, in matters of improvisation, I was becoming my father's son.

Despite the many shortages and post-war deprivations, our family life in Hohnsen moved along quite normally until one day I fell ill with diphtheria, the highly contagious and potentially deadly disease.

Fortunately, diphtheria is treatable by vaccination and our family doctor managed to procure the dosage that saved my life. My mother had herself survived diphtheria as a child and was therefore immune to infection and able to nurse me at our home.

I suppose our family might have eventually settled permanently in West Germany had not my medical isolation, being confined at home with Nadja, caused Oskar to take up residence at a local inn. There he happened to meet Waltraut, the woman who would become his second wife.

Nadja soon discovered Oskar's infidelity, causing their marriage to disintegrate. Deeply wounded and now separated, Mama became determined to take herself and me as far from her unhappiness, Europe and the Soviet menace, as she could possibly manage.

In the meantime, we learned that the ancient Greek word 'holocaust' had taken a new and terrible meaning. The systematic, State-imposed persecution and mass murder, between 1933 and 1945, of some six million German and European Jews, as well as some five million dissenters and others, was repugnant to us, almost beyond belief.

My gentle mother and I could both see that our German neighbours were mostly responding to the evidence of Nazi atrocities with an attitude of self-justification and a practice of mentioning them as little as possible.

Accordingly, in 1949, Nadja and I chose to abandon Germany, Hohnsen and my father Oskar for 'Lager Kosciuszko', a British DP (Displaced Persons) Camp in the city of Hanover.

*The reputable Schiller-Gymnasium school in Hameln, Lower Saxony.*

*Displaced — A Modern Baltic Saga.*

## 4.2 Emigrants

*SS Fairsea, a former troop ship, refitted for carrying migrants in 1949, provided spartan accommodation for around 1,800 passengers.*

At the Displaced Persons Camp, Nadja applied for the two of us to migrate to Australia, a remote continent we considered as far-removed as we could imagine, both geographically and philosophically, from Stalin's ruthless dictatorship and the lingering remnants of Nazi ambition.

The Australian Government was encouraging immigration and we became part of a massive European exodus that would eventually transform the demographics of our destination.

We found ourselves aboard the former troopship SS Fairsea, along with a large number of other European emigrants, including many Poles and Latvians. Our five-week voyage was to be by the shortest route to the South Lands, via the Suez Canal.

Stopovers on this voyage included Port Said in Egypt, Port Aden in what is now Yemen, Colombo in what in those days was called Ceylon, and over the Indian Ocean to disembark at the Port of Melbourne, in the Australian State of Victoria.

The SS Fairsea had a multifarious history. USA-built in the 1930s as a civilian freighter and passenger ship, in 1941 she was converted to an escort aircraft carrier and commissioned into Britain's Royal Navy as HMS Charger, later transferring to the Pacific as USS Charger. After the war she served briefly as a troop carrier, before being fitted out in 1949 for carrying sponsored migrants to Australia and other British Dominions, including Canada and New Zealand. Our voyage carried around 1,800 displaced persons and refugees, mostly from Northern Europe.

As a former troop carrier, our variant of the Fairsea was determinedly deficient in luxury. There were no passenger 'cabins' as such, merely large open spaces with military-style triple bunks, so cramped you could barely sit up in them. I was assigned to a section for male passengers, Nadja to another with the females. The male toilet and showering facilities were one long space, and everywhere it seemed, perhaps due to the frequent clean-ups from seasickness, lingered the unmistakable odour of bleach.

The numerous on-board discomforts, which many passengers complained about, were nothing to a young fellow who had spent part of his life inhaling clouds of burning toast smoke; cramped, hungry, cold and occasionally terrified on the front seat of a small sedan, bumping along through a life-threatening war zone.

On-board ship, I was free to roam and find my sea legs, associate with the other passengers, enjoy the plain but plentiful diet, and fully explore our Spartan surroundings.

My poor mother meanwhile spent most of the voyage in her cramped quarters, prostrate with seasickness. I found myself more-or-less solo on a voyage to the world's farthest shore.

I did not appreciate it at the time, but I am sure those weeks at sea were the beginning of my transition to self-reliance. The sights and sounds of the sunny voyage captivated me. After the many tribulations of my short life — what a wonderful change!

Five weeks on board seemed more than enough, however. By the end I'm sure that every one of the 1,800 passengers were, like me, desperately keen to reach our destination.

Port Phillip Bay, the entrance to the Port of Melbourne, had most of us cramming the ship's railings for a first glimpse of our new land. Our eventual docking was anticlimactic however, occurring well after dark.

By morning, I was practically agog with anticipation of the adventures I felt sure lay ahead. With much to prepare, it was almost lunchtime before I made my way to the ship's forward cargo hold to watch our luggage being unloaded, hoping for my first encounter with our new land's native inhabitants.

I was astonished to discover that only a small part of our allotted team of *wharfies* seemed engaged in the unloading work, and that most seemed

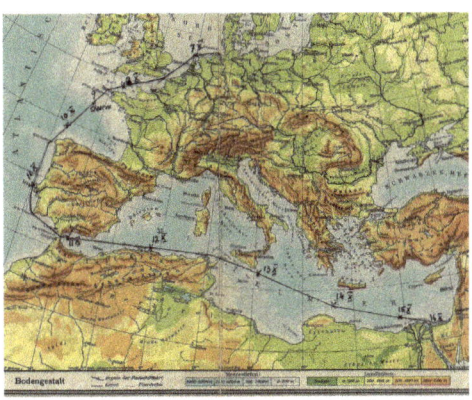

*The voyage from Germany to the Suez, faithfully recorded in Juris's schoolboy atlas.*

to be crowding the solid guardrail near the ship's bows, deeply engrossed.

Intrigued, I edged casually closer to this group, some of whom appeared to be studying printed pamphlets. All were paying close attention to an agitated male voice, shouting in a rising staccato from the speaker of a portable radio.

I believed I already knew about excitable orators, having previously heard a few of the broadcast tirades of Germany's lately departed Führer.

This spruiker seemed to be rapidly babbling in an incomprehensible language, to the accompaniment from his enraptured audience of a growing chorus of exclamations, exhortations, shouts, curses and cheers.

"Pardon me, sir," I enquired of the nearest flush-faced congregation member, after the collective excitement had inexplicably abated, "What is this religion you are practicing?"

"Religion? What bloody religion?" the man exclaimed. "It's the '*orses* yer flamin' *drongo*! You know, the gee-gees?"

Helpfully, the man mimmicked the actions of a crouching jockey, urging his mount to a photo-finish — as if I'd only just been washed ashore with the incoming tide. Which, in a sense, I had.

*Welcome to Australia, Juris!*

*Displaced – A Modern Baltic Saga.*

Soon afterwards, reunited with our sparse belongings and my anxious mother, we "New Australians" (as we were known) were rounded up, documented and transported by bus to Bonegilla, a former military camp around 350 kms inland; our first place of residence in our new country.

Along the way I was struck by the vast, peaceful, wide-open spaces, the sun browned inhabitants, the broad brightness of the sky, the warmth, the plentiful food, and our first glimpses of Australian towns, bushland, birds, and even marsupials.

What an engaging parade!

Engrossed by the views passing the windows of our bus, I remarked to Mama, who incidentally was looking slimmer, more lovely and much relieved to be back on dry land, that we must have surely arrived at the most wonderful place on earth.

*European migrants arriving in Bonegilla by bus from Melbourne, 1949.*

*The box bearing the total of Nadja's household possessions, 1949. Lettering by Juris Meija.*

*A typical Australian pastoral scene.*

## 4.3  A Fishy Beginning

Late spring was warming into a sweltering 1949-50 Australian summer when we took up residence at Bonegilla, a former Army camp otherwise known as the "Bonegilla Migrant Reception Centre," in the State of Victoria.

Our first challenges were to recover our wits and our luggage, and then to come to terms with our unfamiliar surroundings.

The buses that brought us had passed through many towns, the most recent being a sprawling, low-slung settlement called Wodonga. My school atlas showed us that Wodonga was close to the Murray River, the border between Victoria and its neighbouring State, New South Wales, about half-way between the cities of Melbourne and Sydney.

Bonegilla was a bland, former wartime facility comprised of many rows of mostly metal huts. The place was slightly reminiscent of the Displaced Persons camps we had left behind in Germany. We reckoned the camp must have once been a temporary residence for 5,000 or more, military trainees.

Mama and I shared a tiny, partitioned-off portion of one Nissan Hut; a rudimentary structure reminiscent of a galvanised steel water tank tipped over on its side. Our modest space, which we accessed through a door in the hut's semicircular end wall, seemed barely large enough to accommodate our two narrow, wire-based beds.

The camp's huts were neatly aligned in groups or "blocks," each with its own ablution, messing (or eating) and kitchen facilities. In terms of companionship, we were far from alone, with many hundreds of displaced persons from every corner of Europe to keep us company.

For me, perhaps the camp's most agreeable feature was the food, served Army-style in the communal dining halls — plain, plentiful and nutritious.

As somewhere to call home however, the kindest thing you could say about Bonegilla was that it provided us with shelter, having doubtless been designed to encourage its residents to move on and out of the place, as rapidly as possible.

*A Nissen Hut, like those originally deployed as wartime military accommodation in Bonegilla.*

Our first impression of Australian life was of general dryness, dust and warmth. I relished the sunshine, but Nadja suffered badly in the heat.

No doubt compounding Nadja's physical discomforts would have been her concern for our future, the absence of creature comforts, the dearth of cultural stimulation and the persistence of the flies. While Nadja sat around fretting and fanning however, I found diversion in exploration.

Australia's vast, bright sky produces a unique light and atmosphere, obviously unlike anything I had ever encountered.

The warmth, the ubiquitous eucalyptus trees, unfamiliar birds and many marsupials, and the broad, open expanses with wire-strung fences — all seemed equally strange and fascinating.

The camp was situated in open countryside some 10 km from Wodonga and close to a main local attraction, the large, artificial freshwater Lake Hume.

I relished the opportunity to swim with other youngsters, investigating our surroundings and of course, discovering the agonies of my first Australian sunburn.

Perhaps driven by some ancient hunting instinct, or more likely by the monotony of our institutional diet, I became fascinated with the handsome fishes I could see lurking within the dam's depths.

On the road to Wodonga, not far from the dam's wall, was a small motor garage and general store, with petrol pumps and just about anything you could think of to buy, not least being my personal passion in those days — ice-cream.

I should mention here that with no income and a government-gifted total of less than three Australian Pounds (or sixty shillings) in our family coffers, treats of any kind were difficult to come by.

Fiscal constraints did not preclude me from dreaming visions of ice-cream however, and I suppose it must have been the 'Oskar' in me that came up with a plan by which I might convert fish-in-the-dam into beguiling ice-cream-treats.

Soon, I was back near the dam wall with a newly purchased *two-bob* (two shillings) fishing line and an earthworm-baited hook. Within minutes I'd landed my first fish, a real beauty, a Murray Cod, which I

offered for sale to passing motorists.

My fish marketing enterprise was an overnight success. Whether customers felt sorry for the skinny migrant kid or whether they were simply crazy for freshly caught fish, I was soon selling all I could catch.

Indeed, many of my customers were happy to pay more than I was asking — in some cases, ten-*bob* (ten shillings), or even a *quid* (one Pound) — a whopping sum for a young fellow in those days. Before long, ice-cream sales at the general store were booming.

My initiative must have impressed the store manager because she soon offered me a job. After that, I was earning regular wages plus tips, helping out every afternoon and all day during busy periods. In this way, our meagre family resources were boosted by as much as four pounds each week. By late December we were making real progress towards leaving Bonegilla — but where to?

All along, Mama had been aware she had a cousin, Margarite Tis (née Arnholds), who had left Europe in 1946 and (we believed) was living somewhere in Australia with her daughter Karina and husband Laimons Berzins. Initially, Nadja had no address for Margarite, but somehow she eventually succeeded in making contact. Before long, we were excitedly aboard a puffing passenger train, heading for our Promised Land in Sydney.

We realised that we were fortunate that the Berzins existed and had prospered since arriving in Australia. They provided us with our first non-government accommodation — a *fibro* panel cottage they had built in Revesby, a south-western Sydney suburb; bare floors, no furniture, *bucket-loo* out the back, but with town gas and electricity connected.

The Berzins' many kindnesses, for which we will remain forever grateful, provided us with all the momentum

*The Berzins' cottage in the Sydney outer-western suburb of Revesby. This style was typical of new dwellings in Sydney's post-war housing boom.*

*(Left) The large, predatory Murray Cod, regarded as Australia's premier freshwater species.*

we needed to begin our lives anew.

Mama and I moved into the Berzins' Revesby cottage. We managed to gather a few cooking essentials, a couple of mattresses and not much else. Nadja found a job as a seamstress close to Sydney's CBD and travelled there each day by train.

I enrolled at a local Government school and experienced my first immersion in post-war Australian culture, such as it was. Juris became *George* and I soon discovered I had a whole new *lingo* to assimilate — *mate, drongo, larrikin, bloke, sheila, reffo, wog, squiz, dunny, blue, crook, chook, ripper, stoush,* and more... *Fair Dinkum, Cobber!*

*Lake Hume, formerly the Hume Weir, is a major irrigation dam across the River Murray.*

*Displaced – A Modern Baltic Saga.*

# 5

PART FIVE

# 5
# Up and Away.

## 5.1 Viva Adelaide

Deeply grateful as we were to Cousin Margarite and her family, for the means and opportunity to restart our lives in Sydney, Nadja was never comfortable in that city's newer 'outer western' suburbs. She sweltered in the hot weather and the multi-stop train ride to and from work each day was a burden.

In addition, although Sydney is wonderfully attractive around its beaches and harbour, it was already a brash megalopolis at a relatively mature stage in its development, with well-established suburban and social hierarchies. Nadja soon formed the idea that Adelaide, the capital of South Australia, was likely to be a more gracious, cooler and generally more propitious environment. So, before long, we packed up our things and were on the move once again.

After a seemingly interminable, three-day, 4,400 km train journey, we found a furnished two-bedroom place to rent in the Adelaide suburb

of Lockleys, on Elston Street between the expanding airport and the CBD.

We were pleased to have progressed to more salubrious accommodation, appealingly located between the city centre and popular beach-side suburbs of Henley Beach and Glenelg.

We were proud of the excellent progress we had made, considering ourselves 'worthy survivors', which is indeed what we were. Mama purchased a treadle-operated sewing machine and began a dressmaking business, working from our new home.

My mother appeared to have been correct in her assessment of Adelaide as a promising place for us to settle. The compact city is the capital of the vast and substantially empty State of South Australia. In those days it was being promoted as the *Queen City of the South*, inviting tourists to winter in its delightful climate. Nothing however in the promotional blurbs was mentioned about the summers, where temperatures sometimes soar to 42°C and more!

At the time, the regional State Government was encouraging industrial development, and many national-scale companies were availing themselves of bold incentives being offered to establish local manufacturing and other industries.

We had fortuitously arrived at the beginning of the State's most sustained period of commercial growth. Adelaide's national significance was starting to take off. Its population size and distributions were transformed by expansion of the steelworks and ship-building yard at Whyalla; conversion of the Salisbury munitions factory into a long-range weapons development facility; establishment of a large share of Australia's burgeoning car manufacturing industry; and development of numerous secondary industries in and around the city.

Naturally, Nadja wanted me to benefit from the best available schooling and aimed for the impossible, to enrol me at Adelaide High, the reputed *crème de la crème* of South Australian Government secondary schools.

We were rejected. The reason, Nadja maintained, apart from her own status as a single-parent divorcee, was bureaucratic snobbery, pure and

*1950s Adelaide did not, in many respects, seem infinitely different from the Riga we had left behind.*

simple. She became convinced that, as displaced Latvians, we fell short of some imaginary South Australian societal status. In those post-war years, the polite term for immigrants such as we were was "New Australians." The more ignorant or perhaps more colourful of our fellow citizens might have referred to us as *Reffos*, or even *Wogs*.

And so it was the coeducational Norwood State High School for me, each school-day morning a roughly 14 km cross-city and mostly uphill pushbike slog from our home. Norwood was relatively close to the city centre, one of its original suburbs.

As it turned out, I found Norwood High to be an excellent school. I was happy that a number of Balts were already enrolled there, mainly Latvians. I also thought our teaching staff were well-educated and good at their jobs.

My Maths teacher Mr Shearer was my personal favourite, being evidently impressed with the level of postwar education we Latvian boys had received, whether in German schools or in the Displaced Persons Camps.

We Latvians tended to excel not only in Mathematics but also in Physics, Chemistry, Latin, German and English too. In view of our performances, I'm hopeful that the Education Departent bureaucrats might have eventually been forced to re-think their prejudices.

Mr Shearer, like me, was a keen chess player. He worked hard to establish our school Chess Club, of which I became a member. We formed an all-Latvian Chess Team to compete with other schools. Ours included a lad named Aivars Lidums, a very good player, and we went on to beat every High School chess team we encountered. We became the School Champions of South Australia, without losing a single match.

After I had settled into life at Norwood, my mother encountered a Mrs Reintals, a Latvian migrant recently arrived from Melbourne. Mama's friend had a son of my own age named Walter. Nadja mentioned I was doing well at Norwood High and that the teachers were competent.

As a result of this encounter, Walter Reintals, a tall lad we called Viva, arrived at my school, an event that instantly transformed my life for the better.

Not that I'd been necessarily aware of it, prior to Viva's arrival I had been exhibiting a personal disposition which my concerned mother referred to as my "sad melancholy." Perhaps this demeanour of mine was more of an overly serious outlook, brought on by the traumatic, disturbing, and tragic experiences I'd been obliged to endure during my brief existence.

These days, doctors would probably acknowledge that undergoing such trauma would have somehow damaged my psyche, in the same way that they might alter the outlook of many others from their experience of war. In particular, soldiers and the like, who were directly involved with fighting, danger, hardship, loss, displacement, death and destruction — a form of mental injury referred to now as PTSD (Post Traumatic Stress Disorder).

Added to this was the breakup of my parents' marriage, the responsibility I felt to 'look after' my mother, on top of the uncertainty and tribulation that doubtless every teenage migrant feels at having left behind everything that he or she has ever known, in taking up a new life and finding meaningful existence in foreign surroundings.

And so it was that "Sad Melancholy George" was waiting there at Norwood High to meet and greet Viva on his first day of school. In the formal Latvian manner, I politely extended my hand.

What happened next was the start of not only a wonderful friendship, but also an uplifting of my general outlook, where my dreary disposition was gradually replaced by laughter, a growing self-confidence, and a healthy, fresh appreciation of life.

A good 20 cm taller than I was, Viva peered down at my extended hand with apparent disdain, at first making no move to respond. Eventually, in a studied rendering of a posh English accent, he spoke, "My dear fellow, excuse me. Please, do excuse me."

From his pocket, he carefully extracted a spotless white handkerchief, which he unfolded and meticulously re-folded. Then, sniffing loudly and with infinite ceremony, he began to wipe every part of his exposed skin — arms, face, behind his ears, and even the back of his neck.

Finally, after carefully replacing his handkerchief and once again,

*Eskimo Pie — one of Adelaide's and George's favourite ice-cream treats.*

*The war brought impacts of many different kinds to Australia, with America displacing Britain as the prevailing cultural and economic influence. The most obvious changes were in products and entertainment, strengthened by wartime contact with US servicemen and afterwards, expanding American investment. Australians embraced many aspects — drinking Coca Cola, replacing Australian terms like 'chop picnic' with 'barbecue', and buying American-designed products from American companies, such as Ford and Chrysler vehicles, and especially 'Australia's own car', the Holden. Jerry Lewis (1926 - 2017), above, was a much-loved, zany American actor, singer and comedian who appeared in many films shown in Australia during the 1950s and '60s.*

exaggeratedly sniffing while wiping his nose on his forearm, he extended his hand with the funniest imaginable look of upper-class disdain.

I burst out laughing. What else could I do? It was easily the funniest thing I had ever seen — Jerry Lewis at his best.

My school-days, and later years with Viva and his crazy antics, saw the very idea of an overly-serious and melancholy George becoming a distant memory — I regained my ability to laugh.

Viva brought so much joy to all of our lives. For example, one day our school Sports master interrupted a lesson in the classroom. Holding up a misplaced pair of shoes, he asked:

"Are any of you boys not wearing his own shoes? Check."

Tentatively, Viva's hand went up.

"Ah yes, you Reintals!"

"Yes sir, I must apologise. I am wearing my brother's shoes today."

The whole class dissolved into hysterical laughter.

My school days were infinitely happier after that.

Thank you, Viva, my excellent friend!

*Adelaide even boasted its own Coca-Cola factory — and look at that price! 4 pence has become $4.*

## 5.2 Our Salad Days

After three more years at Norwood High, Viva and I were both admitted to Adelaide University to study engineering.

Adelaide *Uni*, as it was known, established 1874, is the third oldest tertiary institution in Australia. Its attractive main campus is within Adelaide's central business district, adjacent to the State Library, Art Gallery and Museum.

The university has produced not only many of South Australia's most notable lawyers, medical and other professionals, businesspeople and politicians, but it also provided a fine higher education for many of my oldest and closest friends.

Our alma mater has an outstanding academic record, being associated with five of Australia's fifteen Nobel Laureates, as well as 110 Rhodes Scholars.

I felt pleased with my progress. Despite having grown up in relatively difficult circumstances, I felt no different from other young men of my age, for example in the acquisition of adult trappings such as motor vehicles, these (to most young men) being outward symbols of emerging manly independence.

Indeed, my personal transportation revolution had started earlier than most. While still at school, and heartily disenchanted with the long uphill pedal to school each day, by working part-time in the evenings and on school holidays, I had purchased a 125cc BSA Bantam motorcycle, thus securing both a measure of independence and a more pleasant daily commute.

Later, by enrolling part-time in my university course, I was able to take up paid employment as an engineering draftsman and, as a further spur to my enjoyment of life, traded my junior Bantam for a hairy-chested 500cc Matchless — going from 'putt-putt' to 'throaty roar.' I began to feel more like a grown-up with the world at my feet. Finally, my destiny was in my own hands.

Without doubt, as far as my adolescence, confidence and family matters were concerned, the dissolution of my parents' marriage had adversely affected me. I had understood at a puerile level that my mother could not possibly have forgiven Oskar's infidelity. But in light of the extreme challenges we three had overcome in our flight from Latvia, my parents' estrangement and later divorce was, from my own perspective, an unspeakable tragedy.

My mother's distress aside, the loss of my much-admired father's capable, all-powerful and seemingly omniscient example was certainly traumatic at the time, although in the end it proved to be not too bad.

Abandoning my father in Germany seemed at the time the only sensible path and not one I will never regret.

However, the unavoidable separation left a terrible hole in my heart and, like many youngsters in similar circumstances, I concealed my grief and resentment by feigning nonchalance.

My clever Mama understood of course. As soon as we were settled in Adelaide, she actively encouraged me to write to Oskar, who by then was married to Waltraut, the object of his transferred affections.

Happily, Oskar responded in kind and to my great joy, our mutual correspondence eventually persuaded him to bring his new wife to Australia.

Oskar and Waltraut arrived in Melbourne in 1955 and, having sold their successful transport business in Hohnsen, were able to purchase a run-down poultry farm business near Ballarat, in country Victoria.

The egg farm, being an Oskar undertaking, was soon firing on all cartons, and the eventual sale of that business enabled the couple to establish Ballarat's first genuinely European delicatessen, trading in all manner of exotic as well as locally produced culinary delicacies.

My Mama, in the meantime, had not been idle in searching for romance. Through our cousins the Berzins, she acquired a suitor of her own, a pleasant Latvian gentleman named Harry Sturmanis, a semi-retired engineer.

Nadja and Harry were married in 1956 and together they purchased a house at 15 Castle Street, Adelaide, a few blocks from my university. My room was near the front door, with Harry's son Juris opposite. We four became a new family of sorts.

I should point out that these changes were all happening in the background, over the course of time. There were many other changes, as we gradually embraced our Australian identities. I was of course making my transition to manhood, maturing under the influence of the university of which I was now a very small part, growing up with the shared experiences of new and established friends, and dealing not only with the natural physical changes taking place but also with what we might euphemistically refer to as 'the call of the wild.'

One such change, which ultimately proved to be rather significant,

*Oskar and Waltraut settled in Ballarat, Victoria, where their marriage continued to blossom and gave rise to Sylvia, my beloved half-sister.*

came about because of an externally imposed introduction to military life.

The Australian Government had, in their infinite wisdom, introduced compulsory military service for young Australian men. Known as *National Service* or *Nashos*, I was caught up in it. The Korean War had ushered in a period of regional instability and from 1951, every Australian male aged 18 was required to register for 176 days military training, with ninety-nine of those days full-time, plus two more years in the Citizens Military Forces.

We *Nasho* recruits were given the choice of Army, Navy or Air Force in which to serve, and without any particular inclination towards aviation, I chose Adelaide University's Royal Australian Air Force (RAAF) Squadron.

As potential university graduates, we cadets were considered potential RAAF Officers, so that in addition to the usual military 'spit-and-polish' indoctrination afforded all Air Force recruits, a good deal of our training involved the study of interesting technical subjects connected with flight and flying — meteorology, radio operation, navigation, principles of flight, airframes and instrumentation, engines and performance, and so on.

Gradually, my eyes became opened to the possibility of a career as a pilot.

For our three-months full-time training we were posted to the RAAF Base at Laverton near Melbourne. where one day, some of the other cadets and I were watching a dual-seat de Havilland Venom fighter aircraft executing 'circuits and bumps' — repeatedly taking off and landing.

On that day we had the opportunity to visit the pilots' crew room, where I happened to enter into the God-like presence of the Venom's pilot.

Ever inquisitive, I respectfully asked him what he had been doing and was told something about testing the effectiveness of the Venom's disk brakes.

Nothing ventured, nothing gained — I followed up by requesting if I might accompany him on his next flight, testing the Venom's performance.

I was in obvious awe of the highly experienced pilot and, to my surprised delight he replied "Why not?"

He ordered me to report back with the appropriate flying gear, which I could obtain from the equipment store.

The extraordinary flying experience that followed had me hooked for life.

In its day, the DH112 Sea Venom was a world-class interceptor fighter with a maximum climb rate of almost 6,000 feet per minute and a service ceiling of about 40,000 feet.

On that occasion, the Navy test pilot, for that is what I understand he was, demonstrated the Venom's capabilities to their full extent.

Soon after we were airborne, we pulled back into a powerful,

39 DH112 Sea Venom FAW.53 two-seat interceptor fighters were assigned to the Royal Australian Navy.

near-vertical climb which if it didn't quite reach the Venom's absolute ceiling, I thought must have been very close. High above the earth, the sky appeared a much darker blue and the world's curvature was clearly visible. After several minutes of unforgettable aerobatic manoeuvres, we eventually assumed a normal flying attitude and returned for a safe landing.

It may have been that the pilot had been hoping to frighten the life out of me, but the experience had the opposite effect. I could hardly wait to do more flying and became our trainee Flight's most ardent student.

Sadly for me however, I was soon to discover that a military aviation career would never, for optical reasons, be open to me. Nevertheless, my desire to take to the air never left me, and in later life I managed to find justification for piloting light aircraft as a safe, convenient and time-efficient means of business travel.

On that basis, I eventually trained for and qualified for my Private Pilot's Licence and frequently flew Cessnas, Pipers, and Mooney aircraft for business and professional reasons, whenever I could find the justification to do so.

*A Schneider Single Seat Sailplane being landed by a member of the Adelaide University Squadron at Mallala, South Australia, 1957.*

*My favourite means of self-piloted business travel was the Mooney M20, a piston-engined, propeller-driven, four-seat light aircraft featuring low wings, retractable landing gear and a distinctive, rather upright tail fin.*

*Our marvelous planet, viewed from 15,000 feet.*

## 5.3  Student Shenanigans

Adelaide University was founded on the British 'Oxbridge' model. We students cheerfully embraced the time-honoured English university tradition of exercising raucous high spirits known as 'ragging' — making extensive displays of noisy or disorderly conduct, mostly characterised by a joyful sense of humour.

As budding engineers, we were proud to uphold one of our university's more outrageous ragging groups, of which at that time I was elected president — namely the 'Society for Confining Immoral Impulses Among Engineering Students' (SCIIAES).

Perhaps the greatest of student stunts orchestrated at my SCIIAES presidential behest concerned the Adelaide Art Gallery, which was situated on the same city street and virtually next door to the university.

On passing the gallery one day, I happened to notice that our city's rather self-important artistic establishment was hosting an exhibition of French modernism. Being as a student entitled to free admisssion, I popped in for a quick look.

I was astonished to note that most of the paintings appeared, in my humble opinion, to be rather uncomplicated to imitate stylistically. This, I thought, was an opportunity too good to pass up.

Thus inspired, I raided the SCIIAES cash box for the price of a blank artist's canvas, which I set up near the doorway to the engineering faculty, along with some brushes and cheerful colours, inviting passers-by to 'have a go.'

Naturally, this stratagem proved a hilarious success, as many random students relished the opportunity for artistic self-expression.

Orchestrating the display of our colourful art masterpiece as part of Adelaide's modernism exhibition seemed at first to be a sterner challenge.

*Viva and George, certified master pranksters.*

This was eventually overcome by having a few of our more vivacious female student friends distract the door attendants, while I rearranged a wall space and successfully hung our contribution.

Finally, with the press notified and reporters from the Adelaide Advertiser on their way, I approached the curator to ask why our fascinating artwork had not been listed in the exhibition's handbook. Confronted with the evidence, the confused fellow retreated to his office to re-check his records, while the fourth estate members duly admired and photographed our work.

The following day, our story was featured in the early general news section of the city's leading broadsheet. This publicity caused quite a stir, to the extent that visitor attendance to the exhibition took a sharp rise, our masterpiece being a major drawcard.

By this time, the curator must have decided that our contribution was too valuable an attraction to let go. So, in order to retrieve it, we were forced to steal it back.

The artwork, which in our collective opinion was at least as remarkable as any contemporary example of French modernism, was left to hang in our student common room, where it was frequently admired and critiqued by students and teaching staff from all faculties, for many months to come.

*The SCIIAES contribution (indicated) to the Adelaide Art Gallery's modernism exhibition.*

Meanwhile, of all the meaningful preoccupations of my life (such as passing my exams, building a career and making a useful life for myself), there remained one particular obsession that has doubtless plagued the mind of almost every young man over countless generations — thoughts of the opposite sex.

I had never had a proper girlfriend and as I progressed through early university life I felt a powerful urge to connect with women of my own age, or women of any age for that matter. My presenting problem was that I had no idea of how to go about it.

I played guitar and sensed that my music might be a useful drawcard, however I realised also that a 500cc motorcycle was hardly the ideal conveyance to which mothers might be prepared to consign their daughters.

So, driven by my primal urges, I sold my motorbike and purchased my first car — a 1936 Morris 8/40 which I restored from a virtual wreck. The car, *Fatima III,* is pictured here, parked outside 15 Castle Street Adelaide, where I lived with Nadja and Harry.

It was around this time that I met my very good friend Graham McHugh.

Our RAAF University Squadron Leader Andrews had placed me in charge of a flight training schedule at Mallala airfield. Dresed in my flying overalls and seated casually in a military vehicle adjacent to the runway, I was allocating names and compiling the flight schedule when I was approached by an extremely polite cadet, immaculately attired in full uniform.

"Excuse me Sir, would you be George Meija?"

Taken aback by his formality, "Yes indeed," I replied.

*(Pictured, clockwise) Graham McHugh receiving sailing instruction prior to our first sail in Halcyon, a few of our female friends keeping a watchful eye on us from the beach, and Fatima III parked outside my bedroom window on Castle Street, Adelaide.*

"And who might you be?"

"I'm Graham McHugh, Sir," explained my visitor. "I have recently joined the squadron and I am available to attend training for this one weekend only. I understand that you oversee the flying programme — should I call you Sir?"

"I don't think so, Graham'" I replied. "Are you looking for something in particular?"

"Why yes," he replied. "I was wondering — hoping actually, one might say — if it might be at all possible — for me to have a flight in a glider."

I assured him that a flight might well be arranged and directed him to the Quartermaster's Store, to change from his formal attire into a flying suit.

"Thank you, Sir!"

"That's alright, but please drop the Sir."

"Yes Sir. Sorry Sir."

That evening, after dinner in the mess, Graham joined me with our friend Val Kumess for a drink or two, and so commenced another deep friendship that has lasted all our lives.

Graham and I invented *The Nikolashki*, our teenage routine for

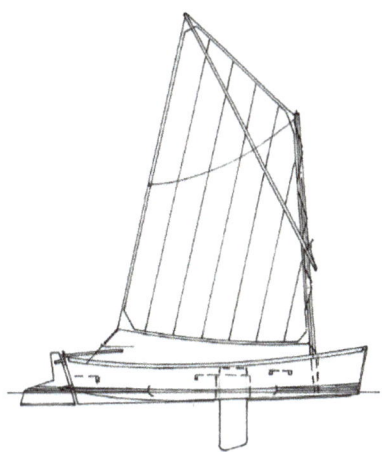

starting a party, involving a shot glass filled with brandy or vodka, downed in a single gulp and followed immediately by a slice of lemon and a measure of sugar. Facing each other in elaborate pose, one of us would raise his glass to a shout of "To Nikolai!"

"Nikolai who?"

"Tsar of Russia!"

"Invented the overhead, underslung, self-emptying dustbin!"

"Huzzah!"

Good times usually ensued.

Graham came from a comfortably middle-class family, while my background was somewhat more self-propelled. Between us however, we were a deadly combination.

Graham had the cash, and with Fatima, I had the transportation.

One evening over a beer, we got around to discussing strategies for attracting the ladies, having concluded that a more compelling ploy may be needed than strumming a guitar.

"What about sailing?" Graham proffered.

It transpired that my new friend had only that day purchased a classic sailing boat, a Sharpie. "All we'll need is a tow-bar on Fatima. We could join the Summerton Sailing club and sail every Saturday."

So that's what we did, and we had a ball. Neither of us had ever sailed before, but after a few capsizes we soon got the hang of it. Pretty soon, it became a case of "Hey George, are we sailing again this Saturday?" and before long we would be swamped with attractive females, each vying to join us for the fun.

We named Graham's plywood Sharpie sailing boat *Halcyon* — after those carefree times:

*Those were the days my friend*
*We thought they'd never end*
*We'd sing and dance forever and a day*
*We'd live the life we choose*
*We'd fight and never lose —*
*Oh yes, those were the days.*

— *Mary Hopkin pop song, 1968*

*Displaced — A Modern Baltic Saga.*

PART SIX

6

Fully Fledged.

## 6.1 Military Madness

My desire to become a professional pilot dominated my RAAF National Service, to the extent that I addressed my flying training with such dedicated enthusiasm that I graduated top Cadet of my course.

Our training produced many hair-raising moments, one example being the day I was challenged by my fellow Cadets, bearing in mind that gliders have no brakes, to judge the landing slide of my aircraft to come to a standstill as near as possible to the open hangar doors.

To the no doubt exquisite amusement of my audience, as I was nervously manoeuvring the careening glider towards the hangar opening, they rolled the doors shut. The glider's nose eventually did stop with mere centimetres to spare, but my horrified face must have provided them with a truly side-splitting diversion.

As a result of having attended a short powered-flight course organised by our Squadron Leader Anderson, where I and several others obtained our 'solo' certification for the Tiger Moth biplane, I was eventually selected as part of a small group to spend time training with 24 Squadron at the RAAF Point Cook airbase in Victoria, with an opportunity to fly the Wirraway, the basic military flight training aircraft of that era.

I had been progressing well and might have continued with an aviation career but to my great disappointment, it emerged that I suffer from astigmatism, a congenital imperfection in the curvature of my eyes. This causes blurred vision, a condition that precluded me from professional flying opportunities.

Fortunately, the Australian Army shortly afterwards offered me a university scholarship which, in return for my commitment to serve 4 years in the Regular Army, provided me with a modest living allowance, on top of my university fees and textbook needs. I was able to finish my 5-year Mechanical Engineering degree in considerably more financial comfort than I had hitherto been accustomed to.

I graduated in 1961 and began my 4-year Army assignment with a 3-month Military Engineering course at Casula in New South Wales, followed by nearly 12 months as a junior Officer in a Field Engineering Regiment, based in southwestern Sydney.

Army Field Engineers belong to the Royal Australian Engineers (RAE) Corps and are commonly known as 'Sappers.' We were trained in and performed a broad range of tasks including roadmaking, airfield and light building construction, bridge-building, field defences, minefield clearance, explosives, demolitions and more. My leisure time in Sydney included sailing in that city's magnificent Harbour.

Eventually however, I decided that life as an Army Field Engineer held too few intellectual challenges and I transferred to the Royal Australian Electrical and Mechanical Engineers (RAEME) Corps.

I was posted to the Army Workshops in the Brisbane riverside suburb of Bulimba, where I was the only living-in member of the small Officers' Mess. Residing right on the riverbank, I was inspired to launch the RAEME 18-footer Sailing Club.

My life in the Bulimba Officers' Mess was thoroughly enjoyable, but sadly, all good things come to an end.

I was eventually promoted to Captain and posted as Officer Commanding the Light Aid Detachment (LAD) to the 4th Field Regiment of the Royal Australian Artillery Corps, based in the dusty south-western Brisbane suburb of Wacol.

In that same year, 1963 and aged twenty-eight, I fell in love and married Rhys Burns, aged twenty-two. Soon afterwards we had two sons, Lachlan and Rowan.

LADs are attached minor units of the RAEME Corps, existing to provide mechanical repair and maintenance support for their larger, host units, in our case one of Australia's operational or combat Regiments of Artillery.

My role was to ensure that the soldiers (called 'Craftsmen') of our LAD were adequately trained and prepared to effectively support our host Artillery Regiment on its pending active service in Vietnam.

Our workshop was meant to not only maintain the artillery guns in the field of battle, but also the Regiment's smaller weapons and vehicles.

At that time, our Brisbane-based Task Force had two such LAD units, the other attached to the 3rd Cavalry Regiment of the Royal Australian Armoured Corps.

I wish to pay particular homage to the dedicated RAEME 'Craftsmen' from our LAD who eventually served in Vietnam. They were not only top-notch tradesmen but also excellent soldiers.

As our LAD's officer commanding, I believe I played a significant role in adequately preparing our workshop detachment for war service, given the minimal level of practical support we received from the bureaucrats at the Australian Department of Defence.

The following is my record of what we achieved, mostly under my personal initiative, to overcome official intransigence, ensuring that our LAD, and thereby the 4th Field Regiment, were adequately prepared for the operational conditions they would face in Vietnam.

The Regiment was equipped with M2A2 105mm howitzers; vehicle-towed field artillery pieces that in the Vietnam theatre were moved extensively by Heavy Lift Helicopters.

Rapid deployment was a key tactic in Vietnam, meaning that the guns, gunners, vehicles, ancillary equipment, ammunition and our workshop had to be relocatable by air at short notice, ready for action within ten minutes of being delivered to a new position.

Such artillery deployments could be expected day or night, in all weather conditions. To support these tactics, our craftsmen and equipment had to be commensurately deployable, meaning that craftsmen, vehicles and trailers with their hundreds of tools, spare

*An Australian howitzer being airlifted by CH-47 Chinook helicopter, Vietnam.*

parts and pieces of equipment had to be constantly ready for rapid deployment.

The officials at Canberra's Department of Defence appeared not to have grasped this fundamental requirement, because much of the equipment they had issued was unfit for purpose.

In dealing with this, I learned quite quickly that lateral thinking is essential to overcome the constraints of bureaucratic process.

For example, official regulations precluded us from refitting vehicles with new tyres because, as it was written, vehicle tyres could not be changed with less than 40,000 km of wear.

Reluctant to send the artillery Regiment to a war with almost worn-out tyres, I felt it necessary to devise a 'work-around.' The system provided for equipment to be declared unserviceable by a special committee, so I convened and presided over a panel that wrote-off some four hundred tyres, and with RAEME support received new replacements.

Another example were the tents issued to conceal lighting and provide shelter for workshops. These needed at least seven men and nearly twenty-five minutes to erect. Also, the field electricity generators, which were so loud in their operation that they might easily be used by the enemy to locate regimental positions.

In appreciation of these and other problems, I turned for support to Colonel Bauer, the senior RAEME officer of Northern Command, an experienced and practical man. The colonel was permitted to authorise purchases of certain items provided total costs did not exceed $10,000. Accordingly, working within that budget, I designed and we constructed effective sound-muffling for the generators, as well as aluminium cover-structures and storage lockers for the trailers and backs of vehicles, with sheltering flaps

*Captain George Meija RAEME with his trailer design housing a built-in desk for LAD office use, with an aluminium body-cover. The standard Army tent shown erected over the trailer remained in the rear area location.*

that exposed tools, spare parts and equipment in a single, rapid movement.

The sound muffling system we built for the generators reduced their operating noise by more than 90%.

I was also able to purchase special tools that proved far more functional than those provided by the Department,

My modified trailers and generators served with the Regiment in Vietnam where the Americans, on seeing them, requested the specifications.

The drawings that were duly provided by our Defence Department obviously did not include my custom modifications, and the Americans subsequently suggested they might be incorrect. Following this revelation, another committee was convened and reported back, "This equipment is illegal and unauthorised!"

Nevertheless, my trailer and other modifications were retained because they were useful in practice.

Our soldiers were trained in jungle warfare to never vacate captured ground — to remain in the battle area, patrolling at all hours without let-up, preventing the enemy from operating near friendly positions.

To prepare my Craftsmen for combat, I introduced measures such as having them bathe their feet in potassium permanganate to protect against tropical rash, dyeing their white underwear green, and so on. I also put them through unconventional combat training, recreating battle noise and confusion as realistically as possible.

For example, with some trickery, our small arms were modified to rapid-fire blank cartridges on 'automatic.' We also constructed dummy explosive devices, such as filling condoms with acetylene and detonating them with a spark from a battery-powered wire.

The resulting explosions were spectacularly loud with a significant flash — thus we staged realistic practice firefights.

We also hammered home the marksman's maxim that Oskar had taught me, long ago: "aim, breathe, squeeze."

That is, take careful aim while remaining as concealed as possible, breathe in deeply, then exhale slowly while steadily squeezing the trigger — an accurate rifle firing method.

We provided these and many other improvements. Much more importantly to me, all of the men under my command who later served in Vietnam returned home unscathed.

Eventually, my 4-year soldiering contract was completed and I was released from military service. A few weeks after that, the Regiment, together with our LAD, was shipped off to the war without me.

*Our Australian 4th Field Artillery Regiment in action, Phuoc Tuy Province, Vietnam.*

## 6.2  Feats of Engineering

After my discharge from the Army, I commenced a career as a professional engineer and businessman.

My first paid employment was with AEI, a major manufacturer of large-scale electrical distribution transformers located in the Brisbane outer suburb of Wacol, a place by coincidence not too far from the Army barracks where I had been based.

The company was a well-entrenched supplier of equipment for heavy industry and the like. My greatest achievement at AEI was to eventually succeed in convincing the bureaucrats in charge of the State's electrical supply, after numerous tedious discussions and arguments, of the superiority of modern sheet coil transformers over the traditional, less reliable and more expensive hand-wound coils in common usage.

However, not being over-enthused by transformer manufacturing, I remained on the lookout for more challenging opportunities. Eventually I applied for and was appointed as sole representative in the large State of Queensland for the multinational, Ohio-based engineering firm, Austin Anderson.

"Austin" had already established offices in Sydney and Melbourne, and my task was to identify, negotiate and execute significant engineering projects in my State, Queensland. This was by no means an easy challenge for a fresh young engineering representative, working an entirely new territory.

My first big break came in Mackay, a tropical city on Queensland's coast, where I happened across information that a prominent local identity named Fred Field was having difficulty working with architects to design the infrastructure and buildings for a new agricultural machinery dealership.

Fred was a frustrated man. His pet project had been dragging on for some months with little progress.

Being brash, confident and eager to impress, I assured Fred that my company Austin would easily complete a satisfactory concept proposal, including preliminary drawings, "in just one week."

"Is that so, young fellow?" replied Fred, eyebrows raised. "I'll tell you what, if you can do all that work to my satisfaction in just one week, the project is yours."

To Fred's astonishment, having burned the midnight oil between myself and our company's interstate design offices, I was back within a week with all the necessary ideas and paperwork, including preliminary drawings and cost estimates.

*The Mackay agricultural machinery dealership we designed for Fred Field, as it appears today.*

True to his word, Fred appointed our company to execute his project — a straightforward undertaking which I oversaw and we completed on time and well within budget.

Flushed with our success, I was linvited to the official launch of the new dealership — a glittering local occasion to be attended by the charismatic then Premier of Queensland, Joh Bjelke-Petersen.

In making his introductory speech, my client Fred made a most flattering reference to my personal role and included an anecdote that began along the lines of, "And not only that, but this young fellow George helped me to make a lot of money!"

*The former longest-serving Queensland Premier, Sir Johannes "Joh" Bjelke-Petersen KCMG.*

Fred went on to describe how, on announcing at his local Rotary club that he'd found a young engineer who would complete his design work 'in just one week,' he had managed to attract a significant stack of $100 bets, all supporting the idea that I would miss the deadline. My eventual success had enabled Fred to collect more than $2,000 in winnings, a sizeable sum for that time, which he donated to charity.

In a massive boost to my career, and no doubt impressed by Fred's accolades, Premier Joh made a special effort to shake my hand and assure me that my company and I would be first in line for future State Government projects.

The first of many projects was soon realised; a lucrative contract to design and construct an expansion of the State Government's Maryborough Hospital, where, to the astonishment of the bureaucrats involved, we completed the work, including variations, on time and $300,000 under budget — a very substantial cost-saving in those days.

Much to my cynical amusement, any satisfaction in our fiscal achievement was promptly hosed down by the evident displeasure of the Government officials, who saw our cost under-run as an embarrassing setback for their elaborate tendering process.

Fortunately, I was able to help solve the impasse by persuading the steering committee to take up their windfall in the form of new X-ray machinery — and suddenly, everyone was a winner.

Perhaps the best practice I gained from Austin was their 'open book' approach to designing, cost-estimating and executing projects, which I still consider to be the most honourable way of conducting business. Perhaps to my own fiscal detriment, I have continued this throughout my life.

Austin was appointed to undertake many large and small government 'design and construct' projects until eventually, through family connections, I found myself at the head of Northstate Engineering in Brisbane, a position facilitated by the retirement of my father-in-law.

Northstate was in the business of panel construction and sheet metal forming. Over the following years we undertook numerous

*George and his company Northstate designed and constructed two of the few buildings that remained standing after Cyclone Tracy had wreaked its terrible havoc.*

projects including some interesting Government remote area work and numerous school and hospital new builds, upgrades and expansions.

Among these were the design and constructions of a preschool and a nurses' quarters in Darwin, Australia's northernmost city. Both buildings were of panel construction and eventually served to illustrate the good sense of engineering design, particularly of structures likely to be subjected to extreme weather.

Christmas 1974 is remembered as the day Tropical Cyclone Tracy demolished Darwin, killing 71 people and laying waste to eighty percent of the city. The scale of devastation was immense, both in monetary terms and in human cost — the ruination of many lives and families.

Because our buildings remained relatively intact, I was asked to contribute to development of a revised building code for tropical applications.

Northstate was eventually sold and for a time I executed high-rise projects back in Brisbane, before forming a new company I named Austco.

I spent the next decade undertaking lucrative State government as well as private developments — hospitals, schools, remote area projects, resorts, shopping centres, high-rise developments and the like.

Later however, due to unavoidable circumstances, this enterprise eventually failed and I was obliged to find a new direction.

Distressing as this was at the time, this powerful event heralded a remarkable twist of fate that was to change my life forever.

*Port Pacific Resort at Port Macquarie NSW, was a significant Austco project.*

*Displaced – A Modern Baltic Saga.*

# 7

PART SEVEN

7

Full Circle.

## 7.1 Return to Riga

The Western world rejoiced in the late 1980s, when the Baltic States of Estonia, Latvia and Lithuania, together with their neighbours East Germany and Poland, emerged blinking into the daylight, following decades of dark subjugation within the Soviet Union. Many Western governments, even those as far away as Australia, were eager to help in whatever ways they could.

I'm not sure how Australian officials knew about my connection with that part of the world, although my security clearance as a foreign-born Australian Army Officer would have provided a good source of information.

The upshot was that in 1991, I was invited by the Australian government to deliver seminars on free market capitalism in the three Baltic States plus Poland, all expenses paid. I was delighted to accept.

I found Riga a vastly different place from the city my parents and I had fled in 1944. To appreciate our nation's new situation, it was necessary for me to gain an understanding of what had happened during the intervening years. Official government sources provided the basis for the following synopsis of the small nation's post-war history.

The 1945 Soviet triumph over Nazi Germany had left Latvia entirely under Russian dominion. An uncompromising Soviet effort soon followed, aimed at rebuilding the nation into a typical member state of the USSR. Harsh political repression was accompanied by radical socio-economic change, including enforced "Russification" of Latvia's cultural life, the effects of which are still evident today.

A 1949 campaign to collectivise Latvian agriculture resulted in several waves of human deportation to Siberia and Northern Russia, involving at least 100,000 native Latvians. This was accompanied over time by large-scale immigration from other parts of the Soviet Union, so that in little over forty years the proportion of ethnic Latvians was reduced from roughly seventy-five percent to around one half.

The immigrants in Latvia provided a disproportionate percentage of foreign Communist Party Members, which following a local movement to redress the imbalance, precipitated a 1959 purge of indigenous Latvian officials. The immigrant elements remained in control for the next three decades.

Relief for the people eventually arrived in the form of Soviet General Secretary Mikhail Gorbachev's 1980s campaign for *glasnost* "openness" and *perestroika* "restructuring."

The first non-official Latvian post-war political demonstrations took place in late 1987, when armed Soviet militiamen were deployed to block hundreds of patriots from openly protesting Soviet rule, while massive crowds maintained a silent, rain-soaked vigil in the streets of Riga.

*A section of the enormous crowds protesting Soviet rule in the streets of Riga, August 1987.*

*The Riga Technical University.*

Later, Latvian youth groups tried to storm the police barriers, leading to violent clashes and arrests but major change was already well underway.

By early 1988, the 'Latvian Popular Front' emerged in opposition to the ruling establishment. The Popular Front triumphed in the elections of 1990, and in May of that year the new Latvian legislature passed a declaration on the renewal of national independence. Later, efforts to restore the earlier Soviet regime produced further violent clashes in Riga, and in the aftermath of the failed coup in Moscow in August of that year, national independence was openly proclaimed.

My invitation to assist with the region's transition to a market economy arrived soon afterwards. With an overwhelming sense of pride and gratitude, Australian "George", landed back in the land of my ancestors, after an absence of some forty-seven years.

## 7.2 Mistrusted

In 1991, newly liberated Latvia was struggling to convert from a stagnating, centrally regulated economy, to a viable free market economy. At the same time, the nation was dealing with deeply entrenched Soviet-era mores, a general lack of understanding of the capitalist system and a widespread mistrust of officialdom.

I initially discovered, as a visiting, state-sanctioned 'expert,' that I too was to be generally regarded as an agent of the official machinery, and therefore not someone to be trusted.

This surprising, unwarranted suspicion of me was borne out during my first seminar, which I was asked to deliver at the Riga Technical University.

My task was to expound upon the differences between a Soviet-style, centrally regulated economy, where the government makes decisions independently of business and consumers, and a Western-style economy, where investment decisions, production, distribution and pricing are all determined by the market, through open competition.

A few minutes into my presentation, it became obvious that my audience and I were not connecting. It occurred to me that I should introduce a personal touch to the proceedings, thereby demonstrating, I hoped, my sparkling humanity and good intent.

I began by asking if anyone had a question on what I had covered thus far and was met with stony silence — blank stares, nothing.

Undaunted, I approached a young woman in the front, again introducing myself and asking for her name. Instantly, I realised I had committed a *faux pax*. The young woman shrank down in her seat, staring ahead and looking like she was wanting to sink through the floor.

I realised then that, under the Soviets, being asked for your name by an official might well have been a precursor to something much less than pleasant, so I tried a different approach.

"Look, I am just an ordinary fellow with some knowledge in areas you might wish to explore. I am a native-born Latvian, returned here as a visitor to rediscover the land of my birth and its people, and to tell you about the free enterprise world that you have already entered, and within which, when you leave this school, you will be required to operate. Now, if it helps, I would like to tell you a story."

And so I began, remembering that this was a time before political correctness placed constraints on what we are permitted to say:

"Some time ago, Adolf Hitler, Joseph Stalin and a fellow by the name of Juris Meija, the same name as my own, passed away and found themselves standing before the Pearly Gates.

Consulting his clipboard, Saint Peter let them in, saying they had been expected. He led the three to a pleasant villa and opened the door. "This villa is for you, Adolf."

"Ahem," said Adolf, "Not quite the standard I deserve, but good enough."

Just then they noticed a repulsive, smelly old hag, lounging on a sofa.

"Gott in Himmel!" cried Adolf, turning to Peter. "What is that?"

"Well Adolf," said Peter, "You know you have sinned, so this is your reward for all eternity." At this, Adolf fell down onto the floor, banging his fists, kicking his heels, weeping and wailing.

Peter closed the door and led the remaining two to a second villa, this one almost as luxurious as the first. And there on a sofa sat an even less attractive, even more repulsive old hag.

"Well Joseph, you know that you also have been a sinner, and this is your reward for all eternity." Hearing this, Stalin likewise collapsed onto the floor, tearing at his skin, punching his head and shouting incoherently.

Peter closed the door and led Juris to a third pleasant villa. By this time Juris was feeling extremely concerned, but to his great relief, there on the sofa lounged a gorgeous, well-known movie actress.

"Hello, Peter!" cooed the beautiful creature, "And how are you today?"

And then she noticed me. "Ugh! Peter! What in heavens name is that?"

"Well, my dear," replied Peter, "You know that you too have been a sinner..."

At that, the room exploded into raucous laughter — the ice was broken.

## 7.3 The Boot Factory

My seminars in an around Riga produced invitations to support various operating enterprises, factories and former collectives, in their transition to the new, free market economy.

Some of these interactions involved small operations such as a cake shop in Riga, and much larger organisations such as an electronics manufacturer that had been producing much of the Soviet Union's telecommunication equipment.

A common theme was my exposure to head-shaking examples of what tends to break down under totalitarian socialism. Especially obvious was the hopeless stagnation that results from the removal of economic incentives. Without definitive property rights, profit-and-loss accounting, and price competition, the entire system had progressively collapsed into widespread lethargy and corruption.

A typical small-scale example was a Riga cake shop where, after admiring the items on display, I tried to attract the attention of the shop assistant. The young woman seemed more intent on performing a manicure than attending to me; indeed, she appeared somewhat irritated by my interruption.

The idea that her future employment might depend on her facilitating the profitability of the business was quite alien to her. So, I helped the new owner to teach her employees the art and importance of selling, and the business has since expanded to a chain operation with multiple outlets.

A Latvian footwear manufacturer was another case in point. A reasonably substantial operation, the factory had for decades been responsible for producing a significant proportion of the Soviet Union's leather boots and shoes.

I was conveyed from my hotel to my appointment with the footwear factory managers in a venerable Soviet-era limousine. As we passed through the gates, I noticed a significant pyramid of brown-grey material heaped up behind the factory premises. Naturally, I wondered what this pile might be.

*Soviet-era boots manufactured in Latvia, in this example not especially notable for their style, quality or elegance.*

My curiosity was satisfied after I had won the confidence of the factory managers, in conversation over their traditional *sveikt* (or 'welcome') repast of sauerkraut, sausage and vodka.

Under Soviet control, the factory had been obliged to use cobblers' twine manufactured elsewhere in the Soviet Union. Due to corruption and other factors, the essential waxed linen thread had been substituted with an inferior cotton-based product, resulting in new footwear soon falling apart.

Understandably, this undesirable feature had produced widespread customer dissatisfaction. Eventually, a letter of consumer discontent had been published in *Pravda*, the official Communist Party newspaper, resulting in frantic local Party officials descending on the factory *en masse*, demanding explanations.

The plant's managers had managed to placate the Comrades' angst by plying them with custom-made shoes made from illegally imported German components, but the problem remained; what to do about the poor quality twine?

The solution was as practical as it was straightforward. Under Soviet regulations, the plant and its workers were recompensed from central banking according to specified production quotas having been met. An electronic counter kept tally of the number of manufactured items emerging from the facility. So, having passed through the official Soviet counting device, the product conveyor was extended and diverted back into the plant, where the shoddy footwear was chopped up by a worker with a guillotine. The pieces were then added to the growing pyramid of 'rejected' material behind the facility.

By this cunning method, all troublesome grumbling about inferior quality was effectively silenced. After all, who could complain about rubbishy footwear that never reached consumers in the first place?

We all laughed out loud at this, but I doubt there could have been a more eloquent illustration of the kind of absurd productivity distortions that seem inevitably to emerge within a centralised economic arrangement.

*Pravda ('Truth') was the official newspaper of the Communist Party of the Soviet Union. It was first published in 1912 and continued until after the dissolution of the USSR. Pictured above is the significant edition of 23 August 1991, featuring the return of Mikhail Gorbachev from enforced internal exile.*

## 7.4 Man vs The Machine

My visit to the Riga telephone factory provided a further insight to the economic malaise that had long suffocated the region and its people.

I had been in a happy, relaxed mood when, after a pleasant walk from my hotel, I presented myself at the factory's guarded entrance. Having earlier spoken with the plant manager, I was expecting to be dutifully admitted, but instead was confounded when the guard rudely rebuffed my cheery greeting and sent me packing from the premises.

Fortunately, there was some type of office across the street and I managed to persuade one of the workers there to allow me the use of their telephone.

The factory manager was profusely apologetic, indeed dumbfounded, having expected me to arrive in the manner usually afforded an official visitor — by limousine. Humbly apologetic, he was soon personally escorting me past the chastened security guard and into the premises.

I was told that the stringent security arrangements had been introduced after it had occurred to Central Party officials that a significant measure of the factory's output appeared not to have been reaching the regime's intended consumer base.

Using various means, the factory managers together with the local officials had succeeded in persuading the Party hierarchy that the problem had been pilfering by the workers.

*A 1980s telephone manufactured in Riga, not precisely as modern as tomorrow.*

The new security measures included not only a strictly guarded perimeter, but also a search of the person and baggage of everyone entering and exiting the premises.

Again, the actual problem had been rather more obvious. Equipment was indeed leaving the premises, by the modest van-load in fact, but at the behest of the local Comrades and factory managers, as a means of supplementing their meagre incomes.

To the doubtless feigned perplexity of all concerned, the grey-market trading had persisted long after the security measures had been set in place.

Here was another example of a failure of the communist system, where the deprivation of opportunity inevitably leads to those who are in position to do so, waging a corrupt war against the Party machine.

Yes, the risks had been great, but did the managers regret their actions? Undoubtedly, but the innate human urge to better one's financial circumstances is evidently irrepressible, for socialist and capitalist alike.

## 7.5 A Rocky Road

During those initial years after Latvia's economic re-emergence, my opportunities to contribute were seemingly without limit.

Meanwhile, there were numerous rumours and accounts of private fortunes being made, throughout the former Soviet Union, resulting from the collapse of the communist system. Some of these were by present-day oligarchs and others by various Western economic investor/advisors, who either managed to acquire or were offered substantial shareholdings in the large and often well-resourced corporations they were helping to configure.

I was not one of these. Perhaps because I was less a foreign capitalist and more a Latvian-born patriot wishing for nothing less than the best for the land of my ancestors, I took no significant opportunity to take financial advantage of my involvement in the nation's economic transformation, despite uncovering many opportunities to do so.

Instead, with two local men Smits and Mazais, we established a modest Management Consultancy with the aim of charging reasonable fees for professional business support, and for identifying and facilitating Australian trading opportunities.

Our several consulting activities embraced a wide scope of emerging enterprises and, engagingly for me, often involved enterprise planning and reconstruction from the most fundamental of platforms.

Consider the Latvian fishing industry as an example. In the decades following World War Two, the Soviet Union had re-established and expanded its almost destroyed fishing fleet to the extent that, by the mid-1960s, with around seven percent of the world population, the Soviet catch was around eleven percent of the world's total. Being well-placed to participate in that growth, Latvia had likewise expanded its fleet as the central government had struggled to meet a continuing shortfall between agricultural production and the Soviet bloc's protein requirements.

Liepaja, the last place my feet had trod on Latvian soil as my parents and I fled the advancing Red Army in 1944, had long been one of the nation's most important fishing centres. Under the Soviets, the Liepaja Marine and Freshwater Fishing Artel had transformed into the Collective Fish Farm 'Bolshevik,' which, with around two thousand employees and operating over fifty fishing vessels, was one of the biggest and most powerful collective fish farms in Latvia, a major contributor to the total Soviet fishing catch.

My modest contribution to former collective industries such as various fishing and timber enterprises, was to educate both managers and employees in the basics of free enterprise.

Entire generations had lived and worked within the Soviet centralised economy, resulting in an astonishing level of ignorance or misunderstanding of free enterprise.

Following the collapse of the Soviet system, for example, individual fishing captains had to be convinced that, as opposed to reverting to purely subsistence operations, there were financial benefits to be derived from building a strategic mix of operational elements to form larger entities, where resources, risks, opportunities, and dividends could be shared.

Even the idea of earning dividends was mostly unheard of, and it even needed to be explained that monies deposited in a bank account might not only be considered safely held, but also earn a financial return.

This is not to say that every citizen I met lacked initiative or entrepreneurial spirit. For example, I was invited to dinner in the home of a medical doctor, a pleasant man with a family, who lived in a modest cottage in a country town.

The meal, conversation and alcohol we shared were pleasant enough, and I learned that, despite his years of study, the man's official salary was roughly that of a labourer — Soviet egalitarianism at work.

Later, on visiting his bathroom, I noticed that the doctor had closely strung horizontal rows of wire over his bathtub and I asked about their purpose. His answer was surprising. The wires related to his second job — as a freelance florist.

Each year, he would harvest a good-sized crop of home-grown tulips, which he prepared in his bathroom before transporting them to Moscow.

In Gorky Street, close to the Red Square, he would set up buckets of spring flowers for sale to those members of the 'utopian workers' paradise' who, being more equal than others, could afford flowers for their homes. The revenue he earned from these annual excursions was more than twice the annual income he earned from his practice of medicine. I took his story as another example of that irrepressible human urge to better one's circumstance.

The self-help ambitions of the good doctor were in stark contrast to the

*Springtime tulips are a Latvian favourite.*

lack of civic pride that had evidently flourished in Riga under Soviet rule. The city at first looked run-down and dirty, with buildings in disrepair, paint peeling, rubbish stashed here and there, plumbing and electricity conduits in dangerous disarray, and a strong smell of urine and human waste in many of the city's corridors, courtyards, stairwells and alleyways.

Thankfully, that initial sense of stagnation and decay was progressively eradicated over the years I visited and worked in the region, as the population readjusted their thinking to the restoration of individual liberties, personal opportunity, property ownership and civic pride. During this time, I was also instrumental in helping establish the International Rotary Club in Riga, which was to prove most effective at raising capital for the improvement of hospital facilities, the development of retirement villages and much more.

## 7.6 Fraternity

Not far from Riga's University of Latvia stands a rather distinguished-looking building — the original home of the Selonija Fraternity. These days the building appears rather elegant, freshly painted and in good repair, but it wasn't always so. When I first saw it in 1991, it was suffering from many years of Soviet-era neglect.

Traditionally, such fraternities are German and Northern European student organisations standing for the philosophy and principles of democracy, freedom, free speech, ethical conduct, patriotic values, and more. Through a practice of both free discussion and formal debate, they have long provided a sociable means by which university staff members, students and members can associate and exchange views, providing intellectual and psychological benefits through the promotion of broader understanding and outlook.

While obviously not permitted under Soviet governance, there are well over 25 Latvian University Fraternities in existence today.

Much is remembered about the important role that University Fraternities played in the post-1918 Latvian struggle for independence, not least in the formation of those fledgling military units that temporarily succeeded in driving both Germany and Russia from our land.

I was particularly interested in the Selonija Fraternity because, many years previously while growing up in Adelaide, I had accepted an invitation to join, partially as a way of gaining access to the social and intellectual benefits which such fraternities provide, and also as an opportunity to stay in touch with my Latvian roots. I had subsequently attended many Selonija functions and discovered that all such fraternities play an important role in helping displaced Latvians throughout the world to connect. I discovered that there are similar fraternities in many Western centres, wherever expatriate Latvians can meet and interact.

In 1991, my initial interest was curiosity. The building had looked terribly neglected, but around the back was a well-used car-space and the door to a well-appointed office. Inside the building I met a middle-aged Russian, call him Dmitri, who was suspicious at first, but with whom I eventually formed a friendly understanding.

Dmitri had a fascinating story that amply illustrated the corruption of the Soviet dictatorship, his office being a leftover from the Soviet era. As a young man, he had been sent from Russia to undertake repair and construction work under direction of the governing class. This appointment eventually led him into the sphere of a local NKVD official, who prevailed upon him to undertake a renovation and extension of that officer's personal residential apartment.

The success of this initial project progressively resulted in further private commissions on behalf of Soviet officials, and ultimately to the design and construction of super villas for the Soviet upper classes. These residences were constructed within an exclusive, NKVD-protected walled suburb of Riga.

Project-managed from the backdoor

of the old Selonija Fraternity building, Dmitri's 'design and construct' projects extensively utilised non-Soviet fittings and fixtures, imported via Finland from all over Europe.

By 1970, his team had expanded to include a fully engaged circle of architects, engineers, supervisors and tradesmen, whose sole functions were to build for the Soviet elite — a clientele whose status was obviously much more equal than that of ordinary members of Latvia's egalitarian workers' paradise.

The irony of Dmitri's extensive career in high-end Soviet-era construction was not lost on either of us, indeed was the subject of several subsequent discussions over cups of tea, thus filling gaps in my appreciation of life as it had been under communism.

Virtually from the outset, corruption had permeated almost every aspect of the Soviet system. By the time of the USSR collapse, most State Enterprise managers, such as those of the factories I had visited, had turned either to creative accounting, or to an active grey market. Likewise, the theft of State property, which belonged to everyone and therefore to no one, had been endemic in Latvia since the start of the second occupation by the Soviets in 1945.

As for official corruption, for citizens it had become a matter of either paying bribes or doing without almost every manner of social service.

*The Selonija Fraternity house in Riga where, in November 1918, a general meeting resolved that all active members were to be placed at the disposal of the emerging Latvian republic's National Ministry of Defence. Accordingly, the Independent Student Company was founded. Those young men later contributed bravely, joined by my father Oskar, to Latvia's successful armed struggle for independence.*

## 7.7 Where to, Latvia?

It's been thirty plus years since I answered the call to support my homeland's struggle to return to the proud and independent nation it once was. Economic progress remains frustratingly slow and Latvia remains a minor player on the world stage.

The nation's psyche has been deeply scarred by its exposure to political violence, corruption, oppression and cultural inhibition; multiple traumas that will likely take much longer than my remaining lifetime to overcome.

On top of the four decades of untreated economic stagnation, Soviet social engineering has left its mark — more than a quarter of the still fewer than two million inhabitants reportedly remain primarily Russian-speaking, with an ongoing matter of concern being the continuing influence of Russian propaganda. In 2004, presumably as a means of securing a measure of permanent national identity, Latvia joined the European Union, and soon afterwards ratified that organisation's Lisbon Treaty, establishing for its signatories a more centralised EU leadership, foreign policy and new policy enactment arrangements.

With its modest population, Latvia's small, open economy necessarily remains based heavily on exports. In support, transportation services are highly developed, as are agriculture and food production, timber and wood processing, electronics industries and machinery manufacturing.

Vast, fertile regions remain under both plantation and original-growth forest, with a temperate climate ideal for sustaining the nation's economic cornerstones. Apart from agriculture, food and forest production, emerging sectors include textiles, food processing, machinery production and green technologies. In addition, the region is one of exceptional cultural interest and natural beauty, so that tourism is emerging as an economic contributor, with annual pre-pandemic visitor numbers approaching three million.

Undoubtedly, modern Latvia is very different from the perilously beleaguered nation my parents were forced to abandon in 1944. The road towards the nation's recovery has been long and remains difficult. Despite visible progress, a recent European Union assessment still rates Latvia as the third poorest and most increasingly marginalised of EU Member States. The nation's stagnating economy, together with some evidence of public wastage and lingering corruption, have reportedly caused many Latvians to lose confidence not only in some of the nation's elected representatives, but also in the whole notion of democracy.

For example, despite a large and expanding increase in the gap between rich and poor, no modern Latvian government has yet demonstrated any inclination towards implementing the EU's anti-discrimination guidelines. The nation's taxation regime remains substantially like that of the old Soviet Union, as distinct from the progressive remuneration tax policies of leading EU Member States. Accordingly, poorer Latvians pay relatively more tax, while the rich pay relatively less. Around one quarter of Latvia's population meets the status of persons at risk of poverty, and yet continues to pay taxes. In addition, social services, health care, food support and housing are not always available to such persons. As a result, nearly a quarter of Latvia's economically productive population has left the country in recent years, in search of better opportunities elsewhere.

Notwithstanding Latvia's debilitating legacy, I believe there is cause for optimism. Positive change can be slow to take effect and I make no claim to having instant solutions. I believe the young nation's increasingly entrenched EU membership provides the greatest hope for the future and I remain confident that, in the years ahead, a legion of loyal patriots and expatriates will continue to lend support and encouragement, wherever and however we can.

*(Top) Latvia is a major exporter of timber and timber products, with forest occupying 52% of the nation's total land area. (Right) The modern Riga Markets displaying some of the nation's high-quality agricultural produce. (Below) Riga's towering Freedom Monument is an important national symbol of the freedom, independence, and sovereignty of Latvia.*

## 7.8 The Price to Pay

Bill Browder, someone I've only read about, is an American-born British financier and more recently, international political activist, the founder and chief executive of Hermitage Capital, at one time the largest foreign portfolio investor in Russia. The account in his book "Red Notice," of what happened in Russia in 2008 as his company fell out of favour with the local authorities, serves to illustrate the fate that can befall any individual or corporation that runs contra to corrupt Russian officialdom.

As Bill Browder alleges, a young Moscow lawyer and business associate named Sergei Magnitsky uncovered evidence of massive tax fraud — a group of well-connected Russian officials had stolen a large amount of money, around $230 million. Faced with Magnitsky's accusations, the same officials had him arrested and thrown into a prison cell, with little means of retaining his body warmth. The young man suffered from gall stones and pancreatitis, and spent months shivering in agony, pleading fruitlessly for medical assistance. This corruptly sanctioned torture was intended to make the young man withdraw his allegations, but he refused, maintaining an evidently misplaced confidence in the Russian legal system. One day his condition grew worse. His guards placed him in an isolation cell and there they beat him to death.

What has the murder of Sergei Magnitsky to do with my own story? Between 1991 and 1996, I was a frequent visitor to Latvia, staying for two or three weeks, perhaps twice a year. While there, I worked with my Latvian business partners Smits and Mazais to expand our management consultancy and, at the same time, foster the development of trading opportunities with Australian enterprises. Then, in 1996, my colleague Smits was murdered, an event that remains unresolved. I decided that the Latvians needed more time to emerge from the Soviet mindset.

In any event, there was an additional, personal price to pay. I had been overjoyed with the opportunity that fate had afforded me, not only to further acquaint myself with the land of my ancestors, but also to contribute to its economic reawakening,

In this process, I had been oblivious to the reality that my marriage to Rhys had been slipping away. Perhaps my emotional intelligence was not as developed as my other skills, but it was harshly brought home to me, seemingly without warning, that Rhys had little sympathy for the powerful patriotic spell I had fallen under. I had clearly failed to adequately discuss my feelings with her. Naturally, I cannot speak for my former wife, or to the precise reasoning for her decision, but when I returned home to Brisbane after the death of Smits and my final Latvian assignment, the locks on our house had been changed, and our marriage was effectively over.

*The city of Brisbane, in Queensland Australia, where I have settled, and I am likely to end my days*

*Displaced – A Modern Baltic Saga.*

# 8

PART EIGHT

# 8
# Epilogue.

## 8.1 Quest for Happiness

Almost eighty years have passed since our family's forced displacement from Riga. Today, I find myself ensconced, safe and sound, on the opposite side of the planet.

At the heart of it all, there was the war, the scale and scope of which the world's people had never before experienced. On that basis I'm sure there must be many like me who, because of our respective experiences, have enjoyed lives that might be described as other than ordinary. I'm pleased that I'm still here and have lived long enough to tell my tale, so that other people might take something from my adventures.

Feelings — each of us constantly experiences them on our journey through life — moods, emotions; positive and negative, are the products of our thinking.

I would say, call it good fortune or bad, that my own life experiences have been wonderfully varied.

I suppose I have been both fortunate and unfortunate, to have seen both the good and bad of the human condition, in a great many of its guises.

During my life I have experienced many moments of bliss, a few of both terror and triumph, as well as extended periods of desperate sadness.

'Happiness,' that mercurial state of feeling generally positive and contented, remains an enigma. The dictionary's definition is vaguely circular, and if you search for clearer meaning elsewhere, it seems that every self-proclaimed expert has a different opinion — confirmation of that old cliché, 'we're all different.'

Stalin's ruthless henchman Beria for example, and Hitler's Himmler, or Mao, or Pol Pot, and the rest, apparently found contentment in exterminating millions of their fellow humans.

For myself, I would say that my own personal happiness derives from the following, simple, infinitely more gentle pursuits!

*I was most fortunate to enjoy 20 delightful annual sailing holidays with close friends between 1995 and 2015.*

## 8.2 Relationships

I have been fortunate to have experienced a full gamut of relationships; family; romantic; friends and acquaintances; teachers; rivals; and business associates.

Of these, few delights can compare with the pleasures I derived, for the most part, from each of my two marriages. It's difficult to imagine any greater happiness than the joy of finding that one special person with whom to share your life, perhaps matched only by the wonder and euphoria of holding your baby child for the first time.

*I met Alexandra ("Sasha", above) in 2002. Rhys and I were divorced in 2004 and Sasha and I were married in 2005. Rhys with our sons Lachi and Rohan are pictured below.*

Perhaps because of my early experience of trauma and isolation, followed by that reluctant separation from my hero-worshipped father, and my 'melancholic' period while my mother and I struggled alone to find a new place and purpose, I must have been more than ready for boyhood friendship when Viva came along. The carefree spark that he brought ignited an entirely new persona in me; soon, my self-confidence soared to create a whirlwind of exciting new possibilities.

Adelaide University was the catalyst for much that has taken place in my life since that time. The confidence, skills, and inclinations I gained there have stood me in good stead throughout my life, and many friendships I made there have remained steadfast to this day.

## 8.3 The Finer Things

I know about the finest of things, namely love. It seems to me that I was nurtured within a cocoon of tenderness and unconditional devotion. As the only child of doting parents, I basked in all the encouragement and loving attention I needed to grow confident in my awareness, secure in the knowledge I was infinitely appreciated, cared for, respected and protected. I am convinced that any child who grows up with this kind of love learns to cherish others in the same way and probably to the same extent.

I am certain too, that it was love that preserved and sustained our small family as we wrestled through the terrible consequences of war, and which contributed the most to the maintenance of our hope and eventual survival.

Love's positive power is, like many things, a product of our thinking.

I was indeed fortunate that, even before I could walk, my parents began a careful process of instilling within me a lifelong appreciation of the finer things of life — music, poetry, art, languages, literature, humour, history, tradition, culture and the beauty of nature. Some of my most blissful memories are of the times spent reading on my father's knee, or basking under the close attention of my mother's gentle, wide-ranging tuition, of discovering new worlds in the silent reading of books.

And to this day, for me, the greatest, quietest and most secure form of happiness derives from my enjoyment of these finer things. I have continued to write poetry and enjoy music throughout my life, playing either piano or stringed instruments, and in later years through my involvement with and conducting our enthusiastic Latvian Choir.

*George (centre) after a performance of Brisbane's Latvian Choir.*

## 8.4 Engagement

Absorption within a favoured activity brings its own form of happiness.

As a professional engineer and business executive, I have made an honest living from applying practical and scientific logic, combined, as the years have passed, with a measure of hard-earned life experience.

For me, every working day presents opportunities to devise absolute mathematical proofs, and because the objects I prove things about are abstractions that initially exist only in my own mind, they sublimely follow the rules of logic.

*SNAFU Members enjoying an official lunch.*

Few happinesses are more gratifying than the feeling of having solved a difficult practical or business problem, and ultimately to have made something useful — a reiterating, private excitement that has kept me professionally engaged well into my eighties.

As for other forms of engagement, there have been many. The years I spent as a consultant advisor in the Baltic region for example, although eventually costly, were in my opinion well spent, and at the time a source of considerable happiness.

There have been many delightful opportunities afforded to me by my service as Honorary Consul for Latvia to my Australian home State of Queensland, and I have been a lifelong Member of service associations including Rotary International and the Riga-founded Selonija Fraternity.

Finally, it is likely that most immigrants, traumatised or not, can empathise with the desire to establish a meaningful sense of belonging within their adopted country.

Perhaps it was this powerful urge that drove me to embrace my Latvian as well as Australian connections at school, sport, university, military service, service organisations and (not least) my involvement in the creation of SNAFU, a friendly association that still functions today, over 50 years since I first proposed its establishment in 1969.

SNAFU maintains direction and purpose by way of a formal constitution. Our aim is to provide our limited membership with an enjoyable platform for exchanging ideas and information that may be stimulating, refreshing, or intellectually challenging — for example, by conducting social events where guests may be invited to discuss their particular knowledge or experience.

My twenty SNAFU companions have tended to be lifelong. The typical lunch pictured above exemplifies the wonderful camaraderie that our group engenders.

## 8.5 Accomplishment

Like the proverbial Boy Scout, I've always tried to do my best. In all my travels I owe a great deal to the nurturing influence of my parents, who instilled in me firstly an unswerving desire to seek knowledge, and secondly to strive for the highest objectives that circumstances and available resources will permit.

My mother Nadja remained a constant guiding light until she passed away aged 92, and the all-too-few years I was privileged to bask in my father Oskar's company were perhaps my strongest masculine influence.

There is no doubt that I have been inclined, only occasionally to my detriment, to emulate Oskar's penchant for lateral thinking and unshakeable optimism, balanced by careful reasoning, creativity, adaptability, innovation, willing service, and a predisposition to lead others safely out of Badlands, both metaphorical and real.

For me, there has always been joy in achievement. Few sensations can match the pride I felt in helping to win my inter-school chess championship, or having 'topped' the RAAF Officer Cadet training course, or graduated as a mechanical, military and then civil engineer. Or for having planned and executed numerous high-value engineering contracts, raising my sons, serving my communities and assisting the region of my ancestors.

In balance, I'm satisfied with my life and my achievements. In looking back over my journey, I realise that most of what might be termed my 'accomplishments' were derived in no small part from the friendships I gathered along the way:

*There are good ships, there are wood ships, there are ships that sail the sea.*
*But the best ships are friendships, and may they always be. — Anonymous*

*My thirst for knowledge, instilled in me at an early age by my parents, has served me well. Here I am in 1968 at my part-time-earned University of Queensland Bachelor of Commerce graduation, having previously graduated a Bachelor of Engineering at Adelaide University.*

*In 2012, I was proud to be nominated and accepted as the Honorary Consul for Latvia, for the State of Queensland, Australia. My continuing duty as Latvia's Honorary Consul is to represent the Republic of Latvia at official functions and community events, and to assist expatriate Lats to obtain their citizenship and other official documentation.*

## 8.6  Purpose

Despite the countless scientific and intellectual advances of recent centuries, the meaning of life remains an age-old enigma that continues to baffle the minds of the world's greatest philosophers. For most of us, the search for happiness preoccupies many of our thoughts and actions, yet we often fall short in our pursuit. We catch an occasional whiff of those blissful feelings we seek, but euphoria seldom lasts. We do not strive for misery and disappointment, but it seems that we cannot avoid them.

Surely the reason for unhappiness is that much of those things we yearn for — wealth, relationships, position, health, possessions and so on — are by their nature mercurial, illusory and temporary at best?

In our pursuit, we engage ourselves in various activities, be they righteous or iniquitous, that serve only to bind us more tightly to the material world we inhabit.

Genuine happiness, in my opinion, comes from a different realm, a higher place. I believe that my own life's meaning comes from service — from serving my nation, my community, my life partner, supporting my family, helping others, teaching our children, leading my community of expatriate Latvians, resolving difficulties and meeting my own expectations of performance.

## 8.8 A Final Word

*My parents Nadja and Oskar (seated left), meeting for the first time in 1930, at the farm of our grandparents, near Riga.*

To me, it seems almost beyond belief that seventy-five years have slipped by, since the final chapters of Hitler's war became the catalyst for the largest population movements in European history.

Millions of Europeans, our homes, families, nations and livelihoods irretrievably damaged, destroyed or disrupted, were expelled or fled or simply emigrated away from Europe, hoping for a brighter future, somewhere, anywhere beyond our native lands.

Our destination might just as easily have been America, or Canada, or New Zealand. I am eternally grateful that my mother and I chose Australia, and that we both managed to establish a happy and meaningful existence in this wonderful, peaceful and happy land.

Remarkable too, was the fact that my previously divorced parents eventually settled within a long-drive distance of each other, so that I was able to maintain connection with my father, Waltraut his wife, and my half-sister Sylvia.

Sylvia and I have survived to become the middle-generation elders of a proudly patriotic Australian-Latvian family.

Our children will carry not only the traces of our Baltic heritage, but also the genetic and to some extent cultural influence of our three parents, those remarkably resilient survivors who led us to Australia, and to all that our family has been and will become.

*George and half-sister Sylvia, loving siblings.*

## *My Meaning.*

Juris Meija, 1937

*The shortness of our lives,
No matter how one lives and strives,
Will surprise.*

*I go in peace, content and smiling,
Just like when out sailing,
Harbour welcomes when light fades.
I've tried to laugh at myself, mostly.
The human story a hilarious ride.
My son, my daughter,
Laugh often inside, outside, it is not costly
No matter how it looks in shades.*

*Try hard to be true and honest,
Never lie to a friend or to your companion.
The value of true friendship,
Or the riches of a true love,
Are paramount, irreplaceable, and sacred.
So, when one offers a true
Hand, do not just take it,
But treasure it as no gold can buy.
Indeed, I tried.
Fight all the negatives, like anger, hatred,
Do all you can, with all you have.
I found solace, deep emotion,
When playing, listening to music.
Meaning too in making, building,
Or changing, creating and in fielding.
And, when exploring finding, searching,
For thought and understanding of the universe,
And in answers to the question "why?"
Even though it only raises the
Next ten questions,
And gives realisation that one indeed knows
Next to nothing.
And that all is changing, and nothing lasts.
But gives contentment looking at the past.*

*In poetry just like in music, the
human story is retold,
So read and find in thought, brief pause,
And look at sunsets and contemplate.
But what truly I also will remember,
Is when I helped to ease the burden,
For a fellow traveller.
Yes, that memory is tender,
And with me locked inside.
To have played the game,
Participated.
Discussed, debated, shared and contra.
And always got up after the blow.
Forgiven all, not least oneself,
Learned and tried again,
But not quite the same.*

*To have soared in the clouds
away from the sand,
One's life in one's hand.
Life was never dull or bland.
I tried whilst on this land.*

*And when I am gone,
Will there be someone, who says of me:
"His nature was gentle, and the elements
So mix'd in him, that Nature might stand up
And say to all the world. "This was a man!"?*

*Juris (George) Meija.
March 2014*

## Can Human Nature Change?

We have learned that, during the twentieth century, mankind's evident penchant for totalitarian socialism resulted in more than ninety million deaths worldwide, by various governments, mostly of their own people.

This sorry statistic includes murder by State sanctioned execution, individual and mass killings, deliberate famine, enforced deportation, genocide, slave labour, ethnic displacement, religious persecution and political purges. There is no need to list the names of these governments or their cruel dictators — we remember who they were and the list is long.

With Marxism and other extremes of regulatory constraint once more openly on the rise in universities and political organisations throughout the West, surely questions arise about the nature of humanity.

Are we capable of changing the way we behave, or does history endlessly repeat? Do we have the capacity for intelligent self-evolution, or are we condemned to forever re-enact the tragedies of the past, to ever-increasing technological extents?

www.ingramcontent.com/pod-product-compliance
Lightning Source LLC
Chambersburg PA
CBHW061138010526
44107CB00069B/2976